ABOUT THE AUTHOR

Leslie Brandt has dedicated his life to the Lord and to the church as pastor, missionary, and writer.

After a missionary term in China, he served congregations in South Dakota, North Dakota, Minnesota, and California, and for three years he was a pastor to military personnel in Taiwan and Japan.

He has shared his personal faith, Bible knowledge, and pastoral experience in several bestselling books, including *Psalms/Now, Epistles/Now,* and *Meditations on a Loving God.* His *Book of Christian Prayer* has become a classic in its paper and gift editions. With his wife Edith he has also written *Growing Together,* a book of prayers for husbands and wives. Another book, *Bible Readings for Troubled Times,* is scheduled for later publication.

Recently retired in Kula, Hawaii, Leslie continues to write and to serve area churches.

Bible Readings
FOR
THE RETIRED

Bible Readings

FOR
THE RETIRED

•

Leslie F. Brandt

AUGSBURG Publishing House • Minneapolis

Library of Congress Cataloging in Publication Data

Brandt, Leslie F.
  BIBLE READINGS FOR THE RETIRED.

  1. Bible. O.T. Psalms—Meditations. 2. Aged—
Prayer-books and devotions—English. I. Title.
BS1430.4.B665 1984   242'.65   83-72117
ISBN 0-8066-2061-7 (pbk.)

Manufactured in the U.S.A.   APH 10-0683

     3   4   5   6   7   8   9   0   1   2   3   4   5   6   7   8   9

To Gaylerd Falde and his wife Joan. Dr. Falde, while caring about and supporting me as a pastor, has also encouraged me in my efforts to be a scribe.

PREFACE

I first read the book of Psalms at a very young age. Even at that time they were exciting, though sometimes confusing. In the ensuing years I often returned to them as a means of articulating my feelings and verbalizing my prayers. While they would mean little to me apart from the revelation of God's grace through the Christ of the New Testament, I continue to discover in the psalmists' remarkable insights new comforts and challenges and a satisfying way of expressing my joy in the Lord in my retirement years.

I have for this reason chosen to use the Psalms in *Bible Readings for the Retired*. They do not provide answers for all the questions or needs of the aging, but they certainly reveal the joys and the struggles of the aging psalmists in their quest for life and truth. They are the personal songs and prayers of ancient believers. It is amazing how well they express some of our fears and doubts and our joys as we read and meditate on them.

They are, above all, an excellent means of pouring out our gratitude and praises to our loving God.

■ LEST WE WITHER AWAY

Psalm 1: "He is like a tree . . . which yields its fruit in season and whose leaf does not wither" (v. 3).

Whatever retirement may mean to us, our children and our children's children—and their peers—may generally regard us as on the final glide path. We are deactivated because of our age, or considered as retired if we retain our titles while our contributions are of little significance. Few will envy us unless they are taken in by the "golden years" commercials of insurance agencies and retirement homes.

Not receiving from others the respect that the elderly appeared to enjoy in centuries past and may still thrive on in other cultures, we need to engender and sustain *self*-respect. The psalms speak to all ages and to each of us irrespective of age. As seen through the eyes of the New Testament, the Christian is never retired, only renewed, and continues to be like "a tree which yields its fruit in season and whose leaf does not wither."

There is indeed some *withering* taking place in our physical bodies, but it need never be feared or manifest in our inner spirits. Jesus Christ has made us ageless, and our lives, steeped in his Word and empowered by his Spirit, can be more fruitful and contributive than they were in our younger years so filled with panic-ridden activity.

 Lord Jesus, enable me, as I grow older, to become more and more like you. Amen.

Consider some ways in which your life can be more fruitful in your retirement years.

■ WE ARE IDENTIFIED

Psalm 2:   "You are my Son, today I have become your Father" (v. 7).

Whatever happens to our bodies, there need be no withering of the spirit as our ship nears home port. While the masses about us seek frantically for some sense of identity—who they are and where they are going—we should by now have emerged from that agonizing quest to recognize and embrace ourselves as the redeemed sons and daughters of God. We may have merited little and deserve even less in the three- and four-score years that have passed us by, but the gifts of God's grace have been poured out upon us, and we are fully justified in claiming our identity as his sons and daughters. We now know who we are and where we are going.

We are, through Jesus Christ and the gift of his righteousness, the "anointed" of the Lord. While our pride and glory is in our Father and God, we can revel and rejoice in God's grace and the eternal peace that it grants to us.

We may be retired, but we are better off than we have ever been. Despite the physical weaknesses and pains that come our way, let us enjoy it.

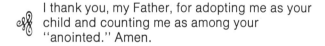 I thank you, my Father, for adopting me as your child and counting me as among your "anointed." Amen.

Today say to yourself: "*I* am a child of God." Think about what that means in your life now.

■ WE ARE SECURE

Psalm 3: "You are a shield around me, O Lord . . ." (v. 3).

While we have been liberated from some of the pressures that continue to harass younger citizens, such as commuting and punching time clocks, we are still plagued by many of the demons that hounded us throughout most of our lives. In addition to the temptations of pride, lust, impatience, greed, and worry, there are added loneliness, depression, insecurity, fear, and doubt.

Our Lord does not promise to deliver us from all these buzzards that hover over us. We have associated with most of them for as long as we can remember. They are not likely to go away now. But the grace of God can render them harmless. This grace is our shield to ward them off, to keep them from mutilating us. Retirement is no bed of roses, but our faith will enable us to lie down and sleep . . . and wake again, because the Lord sustains us.

Nor does our God secure us against the threat of ravishing disease or the possibility of nuclear annihilation. God does assure us that these tragedies that beset our world and its inhabitants will not come between us and his eternal love.

O God, even while I agonize over what is transpiring in this world, I rejoice in your love and rest under your care. Amen.

When you are threatened by anxiety or fear, repeat today's Bible verse.

■ SOURCE OF TRUE JOY

Psalm 4:   "You have filled my heart with greater joy than when their grain and new wine abound" (v. 7).

The psalmist may not understand the disagreeable happenings that come his way. Neither does he pretend that they don't exist. He accepts them and rises above them with a clear witness of assurance and joy, and exhorts us to put our trust in the Lord.

He discovered, as well, that despite the shortcomings of his life compared to the apparent wealth and satisfaction of many who do not recognize or relate to God, he possesses an inexplicable, far greater joy in his relationship to God.

It may well be that we cannot always "lie down and sleep in peace." Even apart from our own suffering, we need to feel something of the pain and oppression that befalls our brothers and sisters about us. Yet the joy and safety that our God bestows upon us will keep us happy and secure even in the midst of this world's adversities. Such joy is indeed inexplicable, because it is God's precious gift. It ought to be the experience of all God's sons and daughters.

 O Lord, help me to experience and reflect your gift of joy—whatever the circumstances about me. Amen.

Make a list of your present joys. From time to time review it and add to it.

■ THINKING AND LIVING POSITIVELY

Psalm 5: "Give ear to my words, O Lord, consider my sighing" (v. 1).

Even though we "lie down and sleep in peace" as did the psalmist, there are times, before and after retirement, when we face the new day with "sighing." It may be something as minor as a dental appointment or even the boredom of a day devoid of the exciting challenges that confronted us in preretirement days. Whatever the reason, physical or spiritual, it leaves us hesitant about getting out of a warm bed to face a hostile world.

Maybe the psalmist was practicing "positive thinking" as he meditated on the wonder and glory of his God. Though often overrated, there are times when it works and is very much in line with the Christian faith. At any rate, the "sighing" of the psalmist was transformed into joyous faith when he reaffirmed and rejoiced in the abundance of God's love.

The truth is that we abide eternally within the abundance of God's steadfast love. The problem is in allowing that remarkable fact to squelch our "sighing" and convert it into songs of praise and joy. Perhaps we need the determination to practice the presence of a loving God. Regardless of our negative feelings, we can enter each day trusting in God's eternal love.

 God, grant that my faith may be deeply rooted in you and your promises rather than in the possible events of the hours before me. Amen.

Today practice thinking positively about your life.

■ WHEN WE ARE DEPRESSED

Psalm 6: "Be merciful to me, O Lord, for I am faint" (v. 2).

The psalmist knew the misery of depression. This was one occasion in which he really scraped bottom and struggled desperately to rise to the top again. There are nights when we, too, will "lie down and sleep in peace." But there may also be nights when we "drench our beds with tears." There are many things to be depressed about: loneliness, ill health, financial insecurity, the tragedies or near-tragedies that affect our offspring, the conditions of the world in which we live.

There is always something that could cause us to languish. These things can turn the aging process into a veritable hell for those who become entrapped within them. If we focus on the things of this world or the human condition, we will be depressed. But the psalmist inevitably rises above these things to relate to his God and embrace anew his promises. He is assured that the Lord knows when and where he hurts, hears his supplications, and accepts his prayers.

This can be our assurance as well. It may appear as sheer nonsense to the unbelievers about us, but we can commit ourselves to our everloving God and really believe in Paul's statement: "And we know that in all things God works for the good of those who love him" (Rom. 8:28).

 There are times when I am depressed even without reason or cause, dear Lord. Help me to focus upon those eternal truths that will always give reason for rejoicing. Amen.

Print Romans 8:28 on a card: "We know that in all things God works for the good of those who love him." Place the card where you can see it every day.

■ WE ARE SIGNIFICANT

Psalm 8:   "What is man that you are mindful of
him . . .? You made him a little lower than the
heavenly beings . . ." (v. 4-5).

What a magnificent insight spelled out by the
psalmist! And his utterance, though scarcely com-
prehensible, has been verified a hundredfold through
the redemption of Jesus Christ. We are not heavenly
beings but have been made the very sons and
daughters of God. "Dear friends, now we are God's
children" (1 John 3:2). The successes and accomplishments of our active, preretirement years may
have occasionally provoked feelings of significance;
but those accomplishments may appear to be rather
dubious in retrospect, and we are thrown back on
the original basis for our personal and mutual significance—our creation, redemption, and adoption as
God's beloved children.

This should indeed be cause for rejoicing even in
the midst of our "sighing" and "fainting," and should
eventually liberate us from those cycles of depression
that come our way.

We are significant. It's an eternal truth declared
and constantly reiterated by God's Word that
no physical deficiency or human failure, sin or defeat,
nor the opinions or condemnations of others about us,
can obliterate or nullify.

 Thank you, God, for making me valid and
significant as I remain your child and servant
forever. Amen.

**Find the hymn, "Children of the Heavenly Father."
Read it or sing it today.**

■ GRATEFUL MEMORIES

Psalm 9: "I will praise you, O Lord, with all my heart" (v. 1).

Retirement is a time for grateful memories. There are some things we would like to forget, but the mind fortunately appears to screen out most of the undesirable things that we have experienced in the years of our youth and tends to enhance the more positive recollections. Our attempts to recreate the past yield to frustration, but memories of events and people who have enriched our lives are precious to dwell upon.

We are not intended to live continually within our memories any more than larvae within their cocoons. Memories are lovely to return to from time to time, but we must also accept life in the present and face each day one at a time. While we contemplate the past with gratitude, we also look to the future with faith, "certain of what we do not see" (Heb. 1:1). The same God who accompanied and cared about us in the past will be with us in the future, whether it be one day or a thousand. We can indeed afford to praise the Lord with our whole hearts.

 O Lord, my heart overflows with gratitude. You have loved me always; you will love and care for me forever. Amen.

Begin a project of writing down some of your favorite memories. Share some with a friend or family member.

■ IN TIMES OF TROUBLE

Psalm 10: "Why do you hide yourself in times of trouble?" (v. 1).

When summer offerings are low, church bulletins occasionally remind the flock that neither God nor church expenses ever take a vacation. We assume that is true about church expenses; we are not always so sure about God. We may never know the times that God has intervened in our reckless course through life in order to keep us from falling over one precipice or another. We do know about those times when he seems to be out of reach and evil appears to be getting the upper hand.

The mass media, generally concentrating on the ugly news concerning atrocities, terrorist activities, crime, and war, manage to put our everpresent God in a bad light. They raise questions that our faith cannot answer and yet must overcome, like those of the psalmist: "Why do you hide yourself in times of trouble?" or, Why are the ways of the wicked "always prosperous"?

Despite his questions, the psalmist had an overcoming faith. This can also be the faith of a Christian in these times in which we live.

 You have been by my side through the many years of my life, O God. May my gratitude be accompanied by an overcoming faith in your caring presence in the remaining years before me. Amen.

Find another Christian and discuss how you can have an overcoming faith.

■ LET'S FACE IT

Psalm 12: "Help, Lord, for the godly are no more; the faithful have vanished from among men" (v. 1).

It is disconcerting to realize that it is our generation that is largely responsible for the precarious condition of the world today. Whereas we are hesitant about accepting any personal blame for conditions as they are, the powers that were unleashed for human destruction in our youth are now poised to annihilate the major part of humanity as well as everything on this planet that makes life endurable. We grieve not so much for ourselves as for our children and grandchildren.

Many of us still cling to the fading hope that God will somehow intervene—that our grandchildren will continue to enjoy many of the good things that life on this world offers. This is a tremulous hope at best. Our Creator has placed the world in the hands of his creatures; and the fear and greed that has brought us this far may, apart from divine intervention, terminate human existence altogether.

God is our refuge and strength. Our years on this world are preparation for that eternal kingdom soon to be revealed to us. We need not worry about our salvation. In the meantime, however, we need to direct our prayers and remaining energy to keeping our planet a place in which future generations may learn about and relate to their Creator and Savior.

 I fear for those who, in these frightful times, do not know you as their Lord and Savior. I do not fear for myself, O Lord. I belong eternally to you. Amen.

Identify one thing you can do to make this planet a good place to live in the future.

■ THE PAIN THAT PERSISTS

Psalm 13:   "How long must I wrestle with my thoughts, and every day have sorrow in my heart?" (v. 2).

The answer to the psalmist's agonizing question is, "As long as life on this globe continues." The aging process does not increase our intelligence, but it most certainly ought to contribute to our wisdom. An important part of this accumulated wisdom has to do with those pains and sorrows that break into our consciousness. All of us have, by now, confronted and worked through various conflicts and tragedies. We have lost loved ones—sometimes through ghastly accidents or illnesses. Some of us bear the scars of serious illnesses. There have been conflicts and breakdowns in our families. Many of these things have caused pain and sorrow that are never erased from our hearts. And they never will be—in this life.

Yet they need not inhibit or impede the joy that God's gift of salvation brings to his children. They may actually accentuate that joy in ways incomprehensible to us. We may not always feel the exhilaration and ecstasy expressed by young Christians, but even in the midst of our pains and sorrows we know that deep-down mature joy of living perpetually in God's presence.

 I can, by your grace, O Lord, live with my painful thoughts and sorrow in my heart, because you bear it with me. Amen.

Memorize today's prayer and use it when you need strength and comfort.

■ GOD IS WITH US

Psalm 14: "The Lord looks down from heaven on the sons of men" (v. 2).

The psalmist seems to have thought of God as located in a particular spot in the universe. Even today many religious people think this way. But we are not so limited. God came to us and revealed himself to us in the very human, Spirit-filled person of Christ. He continues to come to us and to dwell in us through his invisible Spirit.

Yet, even with his limited insights, the psalmist discovered that there was One who was above and beyond the self-centered squabblings and activities of his created children, that the Creator of the world and its inhabitants cares for that which he created.

God is with us! We live with that incredible truth. While the foolish discredit or disclaim the existence of a loving God, we know by experience his presence among us and within us.

 Thank you, Lord, for the faith which rises above the uncertainties of this life and becomes a glorious conviction concerning your eternal love for me. Amen.

Today affirm: "God is with me." Say it at least five times.

■ GENUINE JOY

Psalm 16: "You will fill me with joy in your presence" (v. 11).

There certainly is no guarantee of happiness after retirement—even for those who assume they deserve it and have ample investments to pay for it. In view of the hundreds of millions of starving and oppressed people in our world today, it is questionable whether Christians have a *right* to perpetual happiness. Does not our faith rather celebrate the act of giving up or denying personal happiness in favor of someone else's welfare?

Nevertheless, the Christian does experience joy. It is not deserved or merited, but God offers it as his gift. The receiving of such joy may well include the denial or the sacrifice of material happiness for the benefit of others. Happy feelings may come or go, but the fulness of joy is forever and is found only in a relationship of trust and servanthood between us and our loving God. We are created by God and for God's purposes. Only God as revealed through Jesus Christ is the answer to our deepest longings. Everything else about us is uncertain and insecure—finances, health, even the love of those who are precious to us. Our relationship to God is forever.

Because we belong to the Lord, we can know fulness of joy.

 Grant, O God, not only that I be filled with your joy but that I manifest it in our broken and often cruel world. Amen.

Think of ways you can manifest God's joy in the world around you.

■ SLIPPERY FEET

Psalm 17:   "My feet have not slipped" (v. 5).

The psalmist appears to be in an arrogant mood. It may be that he was comparing himself to his godless enemies. At least in his own estimation, he was faithful to the God revealed through the law. Is it possible that we still at times tend to regard our relationship to God in this manner? If so, the apostle Paul has a message for us: "All have sinned and fall short of the glory of God, and are justified freely by his grace through the redemption that came by Christ Jesus" (Rom. 3:23-24).

The sad truth is our feet *have* slipped—again and again. The good news is this: our salvation is a gift of God and not something acquired through ethical or "religious" behavior. Even the honorable things we have accomplished and accumulated through the past years are but garbage when measured by the righteousness of God. No matter how many times our feet have slipped in those years, we are forgiven in the redeeming grace of God through Christ.

We need to acknowledge and confess our foot-slippings, to receive God's loving and forgiving grace, and to celebrate daily our identity as God's beloved children.

 Thank you, O Lord, for accepting me as I am even as you seek to make me into what you want me to be. Amen.

**Recall some of the times when your "feet slipped."
Thank God for his forgiveness and cleansing.**

■ WE ARE DELIGHTFUL

Psalm 18:1-19: "He rescued me because he delighted in me" (v. 19).

Many Christians witness remarkable rescues in their lives. Most of us have had a narrow escape or two which we credited to fate or luck or even the special intervention of God. We also remember those instances when God's intervention was frantically sought but never received. It is impossible to prove or disprove God's rescuing in our day-by-day affairs. The psalmist, however, was convinced that God had rescued him from the great evils that threatened him— so convinced that he wrote a song about it.

We know that we are God's redeemed sons and daughters, because of a great rescue. Through the death and resurrection of Jesus Christ God delivered us from the eternal consequences of our sinning. There is no calamity or tragedy, except the tragedy of unbelief, that can cancel that deliverance. God rescued us because he delighted in us.

God continues to delight in us, every one of us, no matter what our age or qualifications, our failures or successes. Even amidst the sufferings and sorrows from which we are not delivered, God will continue to abide with us, care about us, work within and through us for his purposes.

 Help me, O God, to bask in your delight of me as I walk and work within your purposes.

Think back over times when you experienced God's rescue or deliverance. Thank God for them.

■ ACCEPTABLE MEDITATIONS

Psalm 19: "May the words of my mouth and the meditation of my heart be pleasing in your sight" (v. 14).

The psalmist's meditation was one of wonderment and praise. It was most certainly acceptable to God. While the ancient songwriter did his share of sighing, his songs generally concluded with the grand, major chords of thanksgiving and rejoicing. Our great God hears and accepts both sighs and praises from his children. He listens with loving concern to both our hurts and our hallelujahs.

If our hallelujahs outnumbered our hurts, and our praises were louder than our complaints, we might be surprised to discover that our hurts and complaints would become less significant in our lives.

Whether our years of retirement are spent on the mountain or in the valley, in urban or rural areas, there are ample evidences of God's beauty and splendor. A morning walk along a sunlit lane, a long gaze at the stars spangling the heavens, a contemplation of the unfolding blossoms gathered from our garden, a thoughtful reading of Isaiah 40 or Psalm 8, may engender a pleasing meditation. It may even fling off the frustrations and complaints badgering our spirit and allow our hearts to be filled with praises and thanksgivings to our loving and eternally reigning God.

 O God, how full of wonder and beauty you are! Amen.

Set aside time today to enjoy something beautiful.

■ PRAYERS—ANSWERED AND UNANSWERED

Psalm 20:   "May the Lord grant all your requests" (v. 5).

The psalmist was generous in his quest on behalf of his people, but perhaps not very realistic. Whereas God's children can expect such a fulfillment of prayers that are offered "according to his will" (1 John 5:14), God does not grant all the requests we make of him.

God will, however, give us our heart's desire if we are on his wavelength and have risen above our self-centered longings to make his will the primary desire of our hearts. When this happens, our prayers are not confined to verbal supplications, but are often the intercessions of the Spirit himself "who intercedes for us with groans that words cannot express" (Rom. 8:26).

Our retirement years give us the time to meditate and pray—for God's people, for the special persons in our lives, for his struggling servants throughout our world, for the hungry and oppressed inhabitants of this planet, for the elimination of nuclear armaments. Perhaps our Spirit-guided prayers will now accomplish more for us and for others than did the best intentions and efforts of our earlier years.

 I know you are tuned in to me, O Lord. May my prayers rise above my selfish interests and identify with your loving concern for your creatures in this world. Amen.

Pray today for your own heart's desire and for the needs of others.

■ THE SOURCE OF TRUE JOY

Psalm 21: "Surely you have granted him eternal blessings and made him glad with the joy of your presence" (v. 6).

Many people of the Old Testament regarded God as terrible and fearsome. Some may have related to him more out of fear than love. Others discovered that joy and peace in life was directly related to God's presence among them, and their greatest fear was the possibility that he might withdraw that presence.

"My Presence will go with you, and I will give you rest," said God to Moses as he ascended the mountain to receive the commandments (Exod. 33:14). "Surely I will be with you always," Jesus said to his disciples before he ascended into heaven (Matt. 28:20). We will find joy, as well as sorrow, in many things about us: the love of our mates, our grandchildren, our friends, a trip abroad, a family reunion. The source of true joy, however, will continue to be the presence of God. Other things may stimulate or entertain for hours or days, but this kind of happiness is short-lived and often followed by boredom and depression.

God guarantees his perpetual and eternal presence. It is this glorious truth that should make us "glad with joy" during these days and years before us. It is possible for us to turn away from him and even to satiate ourselves with the shallow joys about us; but true and eternal joy lies in God's presence, and he will never leave us. Let us acknowledge and embrace that presence and be made glad today.

 I rejoice in your presence, dear Lord, for it means that I can find joy in even the darkest hours before me. Amen.

Memorize Exodus 33:14 and repeat it often throughout the day.

■ NEVER FORSAKEN

Psalm 22:1-11: "My God, my God, why have you forsaken me?" (v. 1).

Jesus used these words in the midst of his excruciating pain and loneliness. The gospel writers accepted a portion of this psalm as prophetic and referring directly to the event of Jesus' suffering and death. Whatever its prophetic value, the psalm-writer was also expressing his own fear and loneliness in the face of unhappy circumstances in his life.

At times in our lives the psalmist's words come close to expressing our feelings of helplessness and aloneness in our confrontation with adverse circumstances.

Christ's feeling of being forsaken in his dying on the cross was followed by the glorious event of the resurrection. That great miracle keeps hope alive for each of us and proclaims the good news that we are never forsaken despite the tragedies that afflict our lives or the feelings of despair that haunt us at times. The resurrection of Jesus Christ offers us the grace to cope with dark nights and lonely valleys and the assurance that, however ominous the future, God goes with us.

 I thank you, O Lord, for the assurance that wherever my paths may lead, you will never forsake me. Amen.

Choose one of your favorite Easter hymns and read or sing it today.

■ WE NEED NOT BE AFRAID

Psalm 23: "Even though I walk through the valley of the shadow of death, I will fear no evil" (v. 4).

The psalmist who felt so forsaken in Psalm 22 expresses fearlessness and confidence in this amazing psalm. And he did this apart from the knowledge and experience of Easter and the resurrection event that is the crown of our faith.

There is a wall plaque that reads: "Don't regret growing old; it's a privilege denied to many." While we have made it this far, we are nearer to our ultimate demise than we have ever been before. We may continue to fear pain, from the dentist's drill to the increasing discomfort of a terminal illness, but we need never fear death. We are indeed walking "through the valley of the shadow of death." Unless Christ returns in our lifetimes, we shall die. It may be disturbing to think about, and few of us will joyfully anticipate it, but we can be fearless in approaching it. "For you are with me; your rod and your staff, they comfort me," said the psalmist in his analogy of the Lord as his shepherd.

The resurrection of Jesus Christ is our comfort because it cancels out all foreboding and fear in respect to death. It makes our death an important and even glorious event which completes our creation and unites us totally and consumately with our Creator.

 I celebrate, O Lord, the truth that "as in Adam all die, so in Christ all will be made alive." Amen.

If you have never done so, begin memorizing Psalm 23.

■ GOD'S PLANET—HUMANITY'S GIFT

Psalm 24: "The earth is the Lord's, and everything in it" (v. 1).

We tend to forget that this earth is God's possession, not ours. It has been entrusted to us. We are placed here as God's stewards or trustees and are expected to care for it.

We may be aware that many people fail to give allegiance to their Creator, but we too have probably been guilty of treating this world as if it belonged to us. We are a part of that society which accumulates this world's benefits with little regard for others. Our emphasis is on gathering rather than sharing, and we too often use for ourselves alone that which is meant for all of God's creatures.

It is the care-less-ness, as well as the arrogance and greed, of God's created children that is draining God's earth of its rich resources, that is making our air unbreathable and polluting the waters of this planet, that is threatening this globe with extinction and the possibility that it will be rendered totally unfit for the next generation.

While we cannot undo the contributions that we have unwittingly made toward this world's ultimate extinction, we can recognize our failures and begin to live and act as if this world is truly God's possession.

 Forgive my selfish utilization of this earth's resources, O Lord, and teach me how to gratefully and respectfully receive your gifts and share them with others. Amen.

Consider joining an organization that works to preserve the earth and its resources.

■ UNPLEASANT MEMORIES

Psalm 25: "Remember not the sins of my youth . . ." (v. 7).

Alongside those pleasant memories that brighten our days are those disquieting ghosts of the past that flit in and out of our consciousness. They remind us of mistakes made, relationships broken, vows unkept, and especially those people we have hurt in some way or another by our pride, our greed, our errors or foolish actions. There may be some things that can still be rectified or repaired—and should be. But others of our wrongdoings can never be undone.

We can take comfort in the beautiful words from Isaiah: "I, even I, am he who blots out your transgressions, for my own sake, and remembers your sins no more" (43:25), or of Jeremiah to whom God spoke: "I will forgive their wickedness and will remember their sins no more" (31:34). These promises mean that we are completely restored to God; our sins are forgiven and forgotten.

It is well that we do remember them from time to time, because it may help to keep us close to our loving God and open and outreaching in our acceptance and love of others. We need not, however, allow these unpleasant memories to nag us. They are forgiven. As far as God is concerned, they are forgotten.

 I come to you in gratitude, O God, because you have paid my debts and forgiven my sins and made me your child and servant forever. Amen.

Write down some of the unpleasant memories of your sins of the past. Then destroy the paper to demonstrate that God has blotted out your sins.

■ COURAGE FOR THE JOURNEY

Psalm 27: "The Lord is my light and my salvation
—whom shall I fear?" (v. 1).

The psalmist was aware that life was not a flower-strewn path. Despite the rosy promises of some preachers, we have long ago discovered the road behind and beneath us to be narrow and twisted, often steep and precipitous. There are evildoers to assail us and hosts encamped against us, and even loved ones who forsake us. The way is often rough; the days are sometimes very dark.

"Be strong and take heart," encourages the psalmist. We are not alone on life's journey. God is with us, and through his Spirit is within us. And when we emerge from our little caves of self-pity and despair to look around, we discover our brothers and sisters in Christ who are traversing this same road with us. The obstacles that we meet and surmount may differ, but the Lord, our light and our salvation, is the same. We need not be afraid.

"Be strong and take heart." The Lord is our light in the darkness that swirls about us and our salvation from whatever threatens us. He may never lead us on "a level path," but he is with us through every day that we live.

 O Lord, may the obstacles on my path through life goad me in the direction of your will and purposes, and may they mellow and soften me in my concern for others. Amen.

Take time today to thank God for being your light and your salvation.

■ FELLOWSHIP ON THE JOURNEY

Psalm 28:   "For if you remain silent, I will be like those who have gone down to the pit" (v. 1).

Not only is the Lord our light and salvation, he is our strength and shield. We don't have to fear going "down to the pit." We are the redeemed children of God. We are his forever. We need, however, to be assured that we are walking with God and that he is our strength and our shield. And we need, as well, to travel in the right company lest we be "dragged away with the wicked."

To be assured that God is with us, we converse with him in meditation and prayer. It is also important to regularly receive the tangible touch of his presence through the sacramental bread and wine, the body and blood of Jesus Christ. He speaks to us through the proclaimed Word; he touches us through Holy Communion. This makes his presence real and satisfying.

Something else is needed. It is difficult, though perhaps not impossible, to sense God's presence and power if we are totally isolated from our fellow Christians. We need each other; we need to travel with the right crowd, to fellowship with others who are on the same journey. This is what the church is all about. "Praise God in his sanctuary" (Ps. 150:1).

 Thank you, God, for your presence and your strength, for the proclaimed Word and the sacrament that helps to make it real, for the fellowship of your children on this journey through life. Amen.

Today seek out the fellowship of other Christians—in person, by phone, or by mail.

■ GIVE GOD THE GLORY

Psalm 29:   "Ascribe to the Lord glory and strength" (v. 1).

It is not that God is in any way dependent on the accolades of his creatures. God will be God without our praises. We need to give thought and voice to acknowledging his glory and strength *for our own sake*. A standing ovation to the Lord and his magnificent works increases our faith and gives strength to our spirits. We foster bodily health by habitually stretching our muscles and lifting or pushing against other objects. Spiritual health needs the flex and flow of mind and soul, the praises ascribed to God and the proclamation of his great deeds, in order for us to remain healthy and to increase in strength as we sojourn through our final years on this planet.

The psalmist heard God's voice through various manifestations of nature: thundering waters, falling trees, flashing flames of fire, floods, and shaking wilderness. Our personal experience of God's presence comes not through nature's revelations. Only through Jesus Christ and his redeeming love are we enabled to know and experience God's salvation. Nevertheless, we can now discern the voice of God in nature about us and discover ample reason therein for ascribing to the Lord glory and strength.

 For the beauty of the earth, for the beauty of the skies, Christ, our Lord, to you I raise this my sacrifice of praise. Amen.

Find a picture that shows the beauty of the earth. Let it remind you to praise God.

■ WHEN DESPAIR BECOMES HOPE

Psalm 30: "Weeping may remain for a night, but rejoicing comes in the morning" (v. 5).

Perhaps it was never thought of as a conversion, but the psalmist experienced something equally significant. He credited the Lord for delivering him from the grave and for being spared "from going down into the pit." This is essentially what happens to all of God's human creatures who, born in sin, are delivered into salvation and reconciled to God through Jesus Christ.

There has been and will continue to be some "weeping" in the dark hours of our lives, but we live incessantly within that all-enduring hope that "rejoicing comes in the morning." The psalm writer never knew Jesus Christ as he was revealed to us, but it is this same Christ who through his sacrificial death and glorious resurrection guarantees the gift and the hope of eternal life for all who open their hearts to God in repentance and faith.

We can be assured of this transcendent hope even in the midst of our weeping and arise in joy every morning of our remaining years because this hope shall never be taken away from us.

 "You turned my wailing into dancing . . . and clothed me with joy. O Lord my God, I will give you thanks forever." Amen.

Memorize today's Bible verse or prayer.

■ IN THE HANDS OF GOD

Psalm 31: "My times are in your hands" (v. 15).

It is not surprising that we face the years before us with trepidation. The conditions of our world—economic, political, environmental, even our own physical condition or financial status—will at times give us reason for serious concern. We may sometimes be more fearful of living in these difficult times than we are of dying.

The psalm writer felt much the same in his times. He acknowledged his distress, his misery, his many sorrows, his failing health, but then fell back on the graciousness of his loving God. His classic statement, "My times are in your hands," highlights a remarkable faith which holds him steady amid the vicissitudes and impediments that confront him.

Our God is a fortress, a shelter, a refuge. Yet we need not pull out of the world in order to feel safe. We are saved by him and safe in him wherever our course may take us. To be assured of this we need only to commit our lives and our "times" into his hands daily. "Love the Lord, all his saints! The Lord preserves the faithful."

 I am grateful that you have wondrously shown your steadfast love to me. Help me to abide daily in that love and to worry less about what might happen to me in the months or years ahead. Amen.

When you are tempted to worry about the future, say to yourself, "My times are in God's hands."

■ WE ARE BLEST

Psalm 32: "Blessed is he whose transgressions are forgiven, whose sins are covered" (v. 1).

The psalmist testified concerning one of the greatest experiences of his life—the experience of forgiveness. It is an incomparable daily experience, one that sets us free for rejoicing and serving. According to the psalmist, this experience is assured when we acknowledge and confess our sins and when we are open and honest about our relationship to God and our fellow beings.

Not only is forgiveness an ongoing experience in the life of a Christian, but, as noted by the psalmist, so is the experience of being instructed and led in the way we should go. "I will counsel you and watch over you," is God's promise. Much of the world may discard or ignore the elderly, but not so our God. His "unfailing love surrounds the man who trusts in him." We are not only significant in his eyes, we are forgiven, and we continue to be instructed, taught, and counseled.

How blest we are, we who are the children of God! Let us "rejoice in the Lord and be glad."

 We do rejoice, O Lord. Be patient with us when we continue to stubbornly insist on our own way, and forgive us. Teach us how to be open and flexible, faithful and obedient, as you seek to lead and guide us according to your will. Amen.

Before the day is over, make a list of all your present blessings. Thank God for each one.

■ THE EYES OF THE LORD

Psalm 33: "The eyes of the Lord are . . . on those whose hope is in his unfailing love" (v. 18).

The concept of God's eyes on us may not always have cheerful implications for us. We may feel at times as we did when we were children under that strange-looking eye peering out of an old stained-glass church window. The message was: "God knows who we are and everything we do." It was unsettling enough to keep us awake through some of those long sermons.

There was nothing unsettling about the eye of God as far as the psalmist was concerned. He assumed that the eye of God was one of anger and vengeance toward his enemies, but was the eye of love and caring "on those whose hope is in his unfailing love."

"Cast all your anxiety on him because he cares for you," is the message of Peter in the New Testament (1 Peter 5:7). This is the psalm writer's and Peter's message to us today. Whatever the message we get from the sometimes cruel and hostile world about us, and however disconcerting the circumstances around us, faith must reach beyond humanity's weaknesses and sinfulness to the very heart of God. "The eyes of the Lord" are on us, for he cares about us.

 Help me, O God, to put away the foolish anxieties that agitate and confuse me and to rest in your eternal and loving care. Amen.

Today affirm "God's eyes are on me, for he cares for me."

■ LOOK UP—AND LIVE

Psalm 34: "Those who look to him are radiant"
(v. 5).

Our focus on life in our three-dimensional world generally leads to frustration and discouragement. While we see evidence of God at work in the world and through the lives of his children, it appears to have little effect on the world at large.

It is only by the power of the Spirit of God that we are enabled to live effectively and productively in this broken world, to impart something of God's healing love to people whose lives have been splintered and violated by the tragic circumstances around them. Our radiancy and vibrancy have their source in God and his kingdom, his life and Spirit within us. Something often missing in our lives as well as the world about us is life, joy, vitality. "I have come that they may have life, and have it to the full," said Jesus (John 10:10). Despite this world's oppressions and deprivations, that is the life that we are to possess and impart to others.

Those who look to God are radiant. As God's eye is on us in loving concern, our eyes must be on God in adoration and obedience. God is the source of eternal joy. We are the recipients and communicators of that joy.

Loving God, break through the obstacles that stand between me and the abundant life and enable me to reflect the radiancy and joy of living for you and your purposes. Amen.

Today select one person around you and try to radiate God's joy to that individual.

■ THE WAR WITHIN US

Psalm 35:1-10:   "Contend, O Lord, with those who contend with me" (v. 1).

The psalmist was fearfully concerned about his enemies around him. What he may not have realized is rather obvious to the followers of Christ: the enemies within us, the spiritual forces of darkness that surround us, are far more dangerous than are those who hate us or those nations on the other side of the world that threaten us.

It is because of those enemies within us, particularly those that we seem unable to handle, that the psalmist's prayer becomes our prayer. Selfishness, impatience, temper, the various addictions that may entrap us, our covetousness, criticalness, lovelessness, our disregard or indifference concerning the suffering of others, our temptations to infidelity in respect to God or human relationships—these things and others drive us to prayer. We may be able to cope with some of them on our own, but there are those enemies of the Christian faith that require God's grace in order to expunge or keep them from destroying us.

We need never be ashamed to request God's help. He knows the human condition and its weaknesses; he is ever ready to assist us in contending with these pernicious adversaries within us.

 Forgive me, O Lord, for often being content with weaknesses. Enable me, by your grace, to *contend* with them. Amen.

What are the internal enemies that you contend with? Ask God for the strength to overcome them.

■ LEST WE FORGET

Psalm 36:5-12:   "How priceless is your unfailing love!" (v. 7).

It is amazing how the psalmist, who had no knowledge of God's love as it has been revealed to us in the crucified and risen Jesus Christ, and who had no promise-laden Bible to remind and reassure him of God's care, was enabled to sense God's love for him.

Perhaps he perceived it in the remarkable stories of God's dealing with Israel that were passed down to him. He may have seen something of divine love in nature about him—in the heavens, the clouds, the mountains, the rivers, the abundance of good things produced by the land. In any case, he saw and heard and experienced enough to strengthen his faith and steady his hope when times were difficult.

How much more should we, reconciled to God's family through Jesus Christ, recognize and rejoice in the priceless and unfailing love of God! The skies and the mountains, the oceans and the green valleys, certainly reflect that love. The Word of God revealed through Christ, proclaimed through the Scriptures, and demonstrated in our lives and through the lives of his children around us, ought to convince us of that love.

Let us contemplate the inestimable and incomprehensible love of our God. It will make this day—and every day—worth living.

 How priceless is your unfailing love, O God! Amen.

Take time today to reflect on the many ways in which God's love is demonstrated in your life.

■ STOP FRETTING!

Psalm 37:1-9:   Do not fret—it leads only to evil'' (v. 8).

There is plenty to fret about. The things that happen in our world are terribly depressing. Even though the good news of God's love is proclaimed day and night throughout our planet, things seem worse than they have ever been. And the response of some Christians is to cling tenaciously to some questionable interpretations of biblical prophecies concerning Christ's immediate return to judge and destroy wickedness and to make everything right again.

The psalmist suggested a more positive approach to living and aging on this planet: "Trust in the Lord. . . . Delight yourself in the Lord. . . . Commit your way to the Lord. . . . Be still before the Lord and wait patiently for him."

This will not necessarily make the world look any better, but it may make us feel better. It may even result, as it should, in our living the kind of lives and manifesting the kind of dispositions that will give joy and hope to others.

 Forgive me for fretting, dear Lord, and give me the courage to demonstrate your love and fulfill your purposes in this pain-wracked world. Amen.

Today curb any tendency to fret. Instead, turn to God in prayer and praise.

■ BLESSED LONGINGS

Psalm 38: "All my longings lie open before you, O Lord" (v. 9).

It may be a bit discomfiting to realize that all our longings are known to God, that even our sighing is not hidden from him. That was, nonetheless, the conviction of the psalm writer, regardless of the probability that some of his innermost longings and sighings were not admirable. We too have to confess that we long for many things that are not pleasing to God.

We are grateful that God did not respond to nor condemn us for many of the unworthy, selfish, lustful longings of our younger years. Out of his forgiving love he withheld the foolish and harmful things we longed and sought for. He did and does respond to that deepest, most ingrained longing of all, the longing to be reconciled and related to our Creator.

That mysterious longing will never be totally fulfilled until we are released from our earthly bodies to be completely united with God, but such a blessed longing is increasingly satisfied as we spend our remaining days and years following Jesus Christ. We also discover in our day-by-day walk with God the gradual fading out of those lesser, earthbound longings that have harassed us through our lives. God deals mercifully and graciously with those who long for him.

 You know my innermost longing, Lord. May it always be focused on you and fulfilled by you. Amen.

What are your present longings? Commit them to God and his will for you.

■ HERE TODAY—GONE TOMORROW

Psalm 39: "Let me know how fleeting is my life" (v. 4).

It isn't likely that any of us need to join the psalm writer in this prayer. Enough has happened to most of us through the years to remind us how tenuous our clutch on this life really is. According to the apostle James, it is almost transparent: You are a mist that appears for a little while and then vanishes" (4:14). There are no guarantees; each day is a gift from our Creator, and we must take life one day at a time.

Nor do we need to pray, as did the psalmist, "Show me, O Lord, my life's end and the number of my days." We who commit ourselves to the resurrected Lord Jesus Christ know all we need to know about our end; we know that it is only the beginning of that new and everlasting life that is beyond description or comprehension.

We need only to know our Lord, to use every day of our time left to us in trusting him and serving him. We do not long for death; we may abhor it. But we need not fear it. The Christian faith has an answer for this ultimate anxiety, and this is the faith by which we live.

 Thank you for today, Lord. Tomorrow is your loving concern and I place myself totally in your hands. Amen.

This week practice living one day at a time.

■ BASIS FOR BLESSING

Psalm 40: "Blessed is the man who makes the Lord his trust" (v. 4).

The psalmist did not hesitate to enumerate his good works: "I proclaim righteousness in the great assembly. . . . I do not hide your righteousness in my heart. . . . I speak of your faithfulness and salvation." It is quite natural that we rummage about in our memories for those good things we have accomplished. We've done a fair job of rearing our children; we have helped a few people when they needed it; we have fed the hungry who came to us; we have witnessed concerning our faith; we have supported our church.

It is good to recount such activities. Yet the psalm writer knew of something more basic to his relationship with God. God's blessings were not dependent on such activities, not even upon the sacrifices and burnt offerings made to him in that day. God's blessings were offered to the person who "makes the Lord his trust."

Thank God for the times he has used you and your gifts to further his purposes. Praise God for his gift of righteousness through Christ that renders you acceptable to him irrespective of your past activities.

 I do praise you, my God, because you accept me now—as I am, that my relationship to you is not dependent on nor deterred by the activities of my past. Amen.

Make a list of your accomplishments in life. Then thank God that your relationship with him is not dependent on them.

■ AN IMPORTANT CONCERN

Psalm 41: "Blessed is he who has regard for the weak" (v. 1).

One of our contemporaries once said: "Discipleship calls us to a second conversion—to the needs of the world of broken people, broken institutions, and broken systems—after the first conversion of a total dependence on God's grace." While the psalmist was not at this point thinking about conversion, and certainly not aware of the meaning and content of the Christian faith as we have experienced it, he was correlating love and loyalty to God with concern for the weak. He stated that God's special blessings are in some way related to one's loving concern for or consideration of the weak.

The words and actions of Jesus, the writings of the apostles, make abundantly clear this important correlation. Our salvation is truly an eternal gift of God's grace. It is by no means dependent on our good works. There must, nevertheless, be a response to God's grace. Our receiving his redeeming love by faith will result in serving other people as the dispensers of God's love and grace.

It is important that we "consider the weak," not in order to obtain God's blessings, but as our response to God's saving love. And this will most certainly contribute to our spiritual health and happiness in the months and years before us.

 Help me, O Lord, to overcome my self-centered concerns with a far greater concern for the less fortunate about me. Amen.

Think of ways in which you can show regard for the weak and poor in your community and the world.

■ DOWN IN THE DUMPS

Psalm 42: "Why are you downcast, O my soul?" (v. 5).

There will be days when we're down in the dumps. Most often we hardly know the cause or the reason. It may have something to do with a low metabolism, an arthritic twinge, a backache, or just five days of cloudy weather. Nevertheless, depression or despondency is very real and, like the psalmist, we have to deal with it.

"Beholding the face of God" might be an everlasting cure for all depression; but apart from some divine vision or dream that is not possible, and we have to settle for hope and faith. "Now faith is being sure of what we hope for" (Heb. 11:1), and hope sometimes becomes blurred among the shadows around us.

There may be times when we have to talk ourselves out of our little caves of despondency. The psalmist appears to be doing this—remembering those days when he led a "procession to the house of God" and the joy experienced as they worshiped together. The God that was present in the sanctuary, and in those sanctuaries of our past that brought joy to our lives, is fully as present with us today, whoever and wherever we are. Of course our "souls thirst for God"; he is the spring of living water that fulfills and satisfies that thirst. Let us make "glad shouts of joy and thanksgiving" despite our foolish feelings. It may make those shadows go away.

 I pray, O Lord, that the truth concerning your loving presence in my life may overpower my nagging doubts and fears. Amen.

When you're down in the dumps, try rereading Psalms 42 and 43.

■ OUR GOD IS GOD

Psalm 46:   "Be still, and know that I am God"
(v. 10).

Hardly a day passes when we are not made aware
of shaking mountains, roaring waters, raging nations,
tottering kingdoms, and the distinct possibility of the
earth eventually melting away under us. The news
media graphically portray some of these things even
as they happen.

Apart from the natural disasters for which we
refuse to accept responsibility, most of the earth's
tragedies are caused by the greed, lust for power,
carelessness, and sickness of the human race.
Things have happened and will continue to happen
that make life on this planet a fearsome existence
at best.

But there is a river whose streams make glad the
city—or the children—of God. Therein is our hope
and habitation. "God is within her, she will not fall."
God is still in ultimate control of our lives in this
fractured world. He is our refuge and strength.

While we are concerned about those who do not
acknowledge this hope—this presence of a great and
loving God within our world—we need not fear
for ourselves or fret about the insecurities and
uncertainties of this life. God is God of our lives
and destinies, and he will not fail us.

 Help me, O Lord, to cast aside my fears and
my fretting and to live boldly and age gracefully
in the security of your everlasting love. Amen.

**When the news of disasters disturbs you, say to
yourself, "Be still and know that I am God."**

■ SOMEONE TO SHOUT ABOUT

Psalm 47:   "Clap your hands, all you nations" (v. 1).

For many of us, the religion of our youth was somber and sedate. Hand clapping in church would have been close to sacrilegious. This might be due, in part, to our particular heritage, since the biblical writers never held out for a dispassionate religion. Things have changed in our worship practices, but we may still feel a bit uncomfortable among clapping hands and shouts of joy at a religious service unless it is held around a campfire or some other place outside of the sanctuary.

The psalmist sets us free in this respect. While there is much to be said for order and beauty and solemnity in the liturgical service, the worship of God ought to be joyous and exciting. We may not be inclined to change our worship services in church, but might add something to our daily worship of God if we occasionally did some hand clapping and shouting to God "with cries of joy."

God is indeed someone to shout about. Our young friends may think we are a bit odd, and at the same time think more seriously about the Christian faith, if we had so much joy in our relationship to our great and loving God that we were compelled to sing and shout about it.

"Praise to the Lord
the Almighty, the King of Creation!
O my soul, praise him
for he is your health and salvation!"

How could you show more exuberant joy in your worship life?

■ RICH AND POOR

Psalm 49:   "A man who has riches without understanding is like the beasts that perish" (v. 20).

The poor never did have much love for those who were well endowed with property and possessions. The psalmist was equally critical and attempted to solve the rich-versus-poor "riddle." He pointed out that whatever success people may have in accumulating wealth, it is an ephemeral thing, and they can't take it with them.

The problem of wealth is a small problem for most of us. There may be, however, the problem of envy and covetousness that haunts us from time to time. It may be those round-the-world trips taken by some of our peers or the carefree lives they appear to enjoy. The psalmist apparently took satisfaction in the fact that when the wealthy die they "will take nothing" with them.

Our poverty, if that is our condition, is not a blessing—except inasmuch as it compels us to put our trust in the Lord. We have no license, however, either to envy or criticize the wealthy. Neither the poor nor the wealthy will discover the eternal wealth and abundance of the grace that God grants unless they put their trust in the Lord rather than in their possessions—or their poverty.

 It is through your poverty, my Lord, that I have become rich in the grace poured out on me. May my thanksgiving result in sharing that grace with others. Amen.

What is your present attitude toward wealth and possessions?

■ BROKENNESS

Psalm 51:1-9: "Let the bones you have crushed rejoice" (v. 8).

It's absurd—that one's crushed bones should rejoice. Perhaps the writer is using a metaphor to describe a fractured ego or a broken spirit. Probably he is expressing what some of us have felt on occasions throughout the years: brokenness. There may still be fractures in our lives that have not completely healed. They continue to give us pain when we think about them. This psalm is one of the most popular simply because we can identify with its author and know and feel something of what he felt and so vividly describes. He is broken; something had come between him and God. We know the feeling; it still haunts us at times.

Is it possible that our broken bones can rejoice, that our brokenness be transformed into rejoicing? Can our fractures be healed so that we are restored to health once more?

Our brokenness in respect to our human relationships may not always mend or heal. The good news of the gospel, however, assures us that we can be restored to health and wholesomeness again. "A broken and contrite heart, O God, you will not despise" (v. 17). The bones which have been broken do rejoice.

 I have through your graciousness been restored to you, O God. I pray that you will heal the wounds that I may have inflicted on other people along the way. Amen.

Think of one broken relationship in your life. If possible, do something to restore it. Ask for God's forgiveness and healing.

■ STARTING OVER AGAIN

Psalm 51:10-17: "Restore to me the joy of your salvation" (v. 12).

Is it possible that some of us, even after our many years of life, still only exist and have never found (or may somehow have lost) the real reason for living? Do we still flail the air with desire but fail to obtain, run but never arrive, seek but do not find? Do we grovel and grasp at the things of this life only to lapse into despondency and defeat with empty and unfulfilled souls?

It may be that we need to start over again, to experience again God's acceptance and grace. The psalmist sought this restoration to his Creator. We have no doubt that he found it and was once more drawn into the loving embrace of God.

This restoration has been made possible through the redeeming and reconciling love of God in Jesus Christ. It is offered to every one of us regardless of the defeats, the unresolved conflicts, the "crushed bones" and fractured spirits of the years we have left behind.

Our failures will not damn or destroy us if they drive us back to the all-sufficiency of a loving God. There we find forgiveness and acceptance. It is there that we are granted the opportunity and the privilege of starting over again.

 I claim, O God, your forgiveness for the failings and faults of my past years. I seek, through Christ's vicarious suffering and victory over sin and death, the grace and the courage to begin anew. Amen.

Identify one area in your life in which you would like to make a new start. Ask God to help you do that.

■ BLESSED ASSURANCE

Psalm 52: "I am like an olive tree flourishing in the house of God" (v. 8).

It appears as if the psalmist needed to compare himself with the evildoers and unbelievers about him in order to realize his blessings as one of God's children. After all, he didn't have the written Scriptures to identify and secure him. He did the next best thing. He is, nonetheless, right on target when he compares a person's trust in God's love with the man who "trusted in his great wealth."

Whatever his intentions, his experience provides Christians with a beautiful picture of their relationship with our Lord and Savior: "an olive tree flourishing in the house of God." It is a lovely picture of peace and security and fruitfulness that accompanies a right relationship to God. And the psalmist gives God the credit: "I will praise you for what you have done." He offers his thanksgiving to God for his wondrous, resplendent love.

Regardless of our age, our successes or failures, we are far more precious to God than a tree planted in his garden. We have the blessed assurance of his everlasting love; because we are his sons and daughters. Nothing can change that!

 Despite the foolish feelings that sometimes disturb me, help me to live and act *as if* I believe in your everlasting love. I do believe it, Lord. Amen.

Be reminded that you are like a green tree flourishing in God's garden.

■ WHEN WE FEEL TRAPPED

Psalm 55:1-8, 16-22:   "Oh, that I had the wings of a dove! I would fly away . . ." (v. 6).

It's not unusual to feel trapped at times. In our daily-job years we often felt that way. Even now, released from such responsibilities, the feeling creeps up on us. It could be indebtedness or solitariness; it might be cabin fever or the noise and smog of the city. We may be alone with no place to go or nothing to do. We may feel shelved or left out apart from the discipline and the benefits of a regular work day.

The gnawing need to "fly away" is legitimate and natural. The cabin in the mountains or the lakeshore cottage should be available for those who desire to get away for a season. For many, however, there is little or no opportunity to "fly away." They don't have "the wings of a dove" and are compelled to stay within the boundaries of their own yard or farm or city block. They have to learn how to cope with the feeling of being trapped.

Feeling trapped is a problem for many people. It may be such for us. It won't be easy, but we might begin to deal with it by accepting our present, post-retirement circumstances as God's new vocation for us and learning how to grow, blossom, and bear fruit where we are planted.

 I can't solve any problems, Lord, by running away. I seek your grace to deal effectually with them right where I am. Amen.

Make a poster that encourages you to "Bloom where you are planted."

■ WE ARE SUCCESSES

Psalm 57: "I cry out to God . . . who fulfills his purpose for me" (v. 2).

Nagging questions may nibble away at our peace of mind and cast shadows upon these "golden years" of retirement: Has my life been a success? Are there stars in my crown? Did I accomplish anything very significant?

It is helpful to have spouses who still recognize and accept us, children and grandchildren who adore us, but not all of us are that fortunate. And those "success theology" preachers who insist that positive-thinking Christians *will* always be successful, do not add to our peace of mind.

But our great God has fulfilled his purpose in granting his salvation to all who turn to him. He did this through the sacrificial death and the resurrection of his Son, Jesus Christ. Because of God's gift of grace, all who claim this Jesus as their Savior and crown him King of their lives are truly successful.

As we follow this Christ, we continue to live significant and successful lives, and to be the means by which God fulfills his purposes in the lives of others.

 I thank you, God, that in you and because of you, I am significant. Even if I am not recognized by the world about me, I am successful by your standards. Amen.

As you look back on your life, what made you feel successful? How do you feel about that now?

■ WE ARE WHAT WE HOPE FOR

Psalm 62: "Find rest, O my soul, in God alone; my hope comes from him" (v. 5).

We wait for many things in this life—degrees, inheritances, a home of our own, recognition for some achievement, a grandchild to carry on our name, a vacation abroad, the healing of some illness, the time of retirement. The strange thing is that when some of these things do happen, such as our retirement, they are not as fulfilling as we expected them to be.

Whether or not the psalmist discovered this, he concluded that "God alone" was the answer to his many wants and longings.

Even while we abide in God, we wait for him. Our present relationship to him is steeped in hope and faith. We believe we are God's redeemed children, his sons and daughters forever. We live in the hope that our redemption will be fully revealed to us when Christ returns to gather together his kingdom, or following our exodus from this life to enter fully into union with God.

We will not be disappointed in our hope for heaven and its uncountable blessings. And while we wait, we rejoice and continue to serve the Christ who has already reconciled us to his Father.

 You are my Lord and Savior, and while I wait for that which is guaranteed, I continue to be blessed by your loving gifts of love and life and the joy they bring to me. Amen.

Memorize today's Bible verse. Repeat it to strengthen your hope in God.

■ GOD'S LOVE—OUR JOY

Psalm 63: "Because your love is better than life, my lips will glorify you" (v. 3).

Sometimes we think that the joy that God gives us will be in the life after death. Eternal joy and total union with God, an everlasting relationship with him apart from sin or sorrow or suffering, is something we rightly anticipate. We are, however, cheating ourselves if we fail to discover joy in *this* life.

The psalmist appears to have little, if any, concept of life after death, but the psalmist does find in his understanding of God's love a reason for joy even in the midst of his adversities. His praises to God come out of the realization that God loves him, and this conviction is more important to him than life itself.

Our knowledge and experience of God's love are meant to bring joy to our lives here and now—in the midst of our pains and sorrows. Although we are but sojourners here and "heaven is our home," we need not live joylessly among difficult circumstances. God's steadfast love is everpresent. It is this that we should be celebrating and demonstrating now—even before the sun sets on our journey through this world.

 I am your child forever, dear Lord. I celebrate and rejoice in that which I have now and which will always be mine. Amen.

Try keeping a list of the joys you experience each day.

■ WE ARE THE CHOSEN ONES

Psalm 65: "Blessed is the man you choose and bring near to live in your courts" (v. 4).

At first the Israelites had a limited concept of who were or were not among the chosen people of God. Gradually they learned that our Lord's plan includes all people on this planet: "For he chose us in him before the creation of the world to be holy and blameless in his sight" (Eph. 1:4).

We are truly among the blessed ones, the chosen ones, for through Jesus Christ we have been reconciled to our Creator, brought near to him—to live in his courts forever. Even more than the psalmist, we have the knowledge and experience of this act of God. We are "filled with the good things" of God's house.

We continue to live in hope, because the full meaning of being the chosen ones is still to be revealed to us. "You did not choose me, but I chose you," said Jesus (John 15:16). It is this that gives us the assurance that we are indeed the chosen ones and abide with God now and forever. It is this that makes for joyful living and grants us the peace and security that cannot be taken from us.

There are, O Lord, many unsatisfying things about living and aging in this life, but I find satisfaction in "the good things of your house" and in knowing that you have chosen me "to live in your courts." Amen.

Today remind yourself that you are chosen by God to live in his courts forever.

■ A RELIABLE WITNESS

Psalm 66:   "Come and see what God has done"
(v. 5).

In this psalm the writer bears witness for the purpose of drawing others to the great Source of love and joy. He invites his readers or listeners to "come and see what God has done." This is a testimony and an invitation.

It is as relevant in our day as it was in his. We may not be in the position to preach to people, even if we wanted to. But there is nothing more effective in relating people to God than simple, one-to-one witnessing. A Hebrew proverb maintains, "No one can be considered old until he or she has been proven wise." It has also been suggested that no one can be considered wise until he is old. With all the years behind us we ought to be wise enough to become effective witnesses and, by our lives as well as our words, invite others to "come and see what God has done."

Because of the need to cope with the griefs and losses that frequently accompany aging, older people may have more need for spiritual sustenance than do the young. This may be the reason we are still around —to be reliable witnesses to one another concerning the grace and goodness of God.

 O God, make my life a song, an example, a witness, that will encourage others to see what you can do for them. Amen.

This week look for opportunities to witness to your faith in God.

■ A SONG OF PRAISE

Psalm 67:   "May the peoples praise you, O God"
(v. 3).

In this lovely song there are no criticisms of others,
no complaints about the difficulties of living in this
world. It is pure praise, and the songwriter lets it
ring out loud and clear.

There are days like this in our lives. May they
increase in number! Why not dedicate this day,
tomorrow, the rest of the week, to ignoring the
negative, accentuating the positive, and spend our
waking moments finding things to be thankful for.
We may be surprised to discover how much better we
feel about retirement and the aging process.

It doesn't work? Keep at it; eventually it will. God
has blessed us. It is important to him and to us that
we make some effort to count those blessings. They are
all about us. We may be slowing down when it comes
to physical exercise and eventually may not be able to
move very much at all, but our minds and spirits will
be healthy and remain active if we exercise daily in
the act of praising God.

"Praise God, from whom all blessings flow;
Praise him, all creatures here below;
Praise him above, ye heavenly host;
Praise Father, Son, and Holy Ghost." Amen.

**Start a list of the blessings you have experienced in
life. Let it spur you on to praise God.**

■ ONE DAY AT A TIME

Psalm 68:1-20: "Praise be to the Lord, to God our Savior, who daily bears our burdens" (v. 19).

One day at a time" is a popular slogan and a realistic one for the retired and the aging. It was certainly real to the psalmist in his day of vicious enemies and threatening armies. We, too, live in an uncertain and insecure world. We have to take it one day at a time.

The psalm writer looked to the mighty acts of God in nature about him to comfort him in his daily course through life. We are able to look to God's inner presence through the gift of his Spirit to sustain us day by day. The same power that brought Christ into our world through the virgin Mary, and raised him from the dead, is the same power, that divine energy, that abides within us.

We need not doubt that our God is great enough to enable us to cope with the comparatively small problems that badger us from one day to the next. Rather than grovel in our frailties and failures, let us rise up in faith, recognize who we are and what we have become through Christ, and accept each day as it comes with courage and confidence!

 Help me, O Lord, to live each day as if you are truly in control, that you really do love me and will abide within me always. Amen.

This week practice living "in daytight compartments."

◼ NO PLACE TO GO—BUT UP

Psalm 69:1-15: "Save me, O God, for the waters have come up to my neck" (v. 1).

Although we believe we are God's beloved children, we are still at times throttled with despair, at the bottom of the barrel, with no place to go but up.

There are a number of things that can desolate us: our own pain, the death of a loved one, the passing on of friends. "It's no fun growing old," is a frequent comment among us. There are irreplaceable losses, unbearable sufferings, times when the waters come up to our necks.

These things cannot be camouflaged, only accepted, sometimes shared with others, and always committed to a loving God who, while he may not deliver us from these griefs, does feel the pain we feel and promises us the grace to eventually rise above it.

Of this we can rest assured, the floods that engulf us will not come between us and God's eternal love. It is our renewed conviction about that love that will steady our frail crafts when the winds and tides rage around us.

I can't even pray today, O Lord, except to repeat the words of the psalm writer: "Save me, O God, for the waters have come up to my neck." Amen.

When you feel overwhelmed by problems, try sharing them with others—and with God.

■ DEALING WITH SOLITARINESS

Psalm 71: "Do not cast me away when I am old;
do not forsake me when my strength is gone" (v. 9).

If we haven't already learned how to live with
ourselves, we will have to learn in these years of
retirement. We need others; total isolationism does
not enable us to mature as healthy-minded individuals.
The pull and push of interpersonal relationships is
necessary for the development of mind and spirit.

Yet we face our God and the world as individuals.
We cannot ride through life on the shoulders of the
crowd. We have to learn how to be alone, how to
handle solitariness, how to be at peace with ourselves.
We need to believe in God's love and care when
nobody is around to assure us of it.

This learning process is often painful, but it can
lead to a joy and peace that we never realized in the
noisy and busy years of our lives. It will also prepare
us for a more productive and enriching relationship
with others with whom we travel on our journey.

The final event of our lives on this earth is one that
we must face alone. And yet we can face it without
fear, because we are never really alone. We are
children of God. We have a homecoming we will
attend, and our heavenly Father will be there to greet
us joyfully.

 Thank you, gracious God, for the assurance
that you will never cast me away, and I will
never really be alone. Amen.

**Ask God to show you how you can best live with
solitariness.**

■ A COMMON OCCURRENCE

Psalm 73: "My flesh and my heart may fail, but God is the strength of my heart . . ." (v. 26).

Failure of nerve, heart or mind, is a common occurrence in the lives of God's children. Physically, at least, its probability increases with aging. The psalmist was undoubtedly referring to spiritual failure and upbraided himself for it. The proud pagans around him, his enemies before him, the wicked on all sides of him—all got under his skin at times. In desperation and rebellion he was driven to God, and he found God and his love to be his only consolation.

This is the human condition. Sometimes we do rebel and act like "beasts" toward God. Many things— the conditions of our world, people's indifference to God and his purposes, our ebbing strength, failing health, loneliness, feelings of uselessness, the conflicts that assail us—will get under our skin and make us feel like failures.

"But God is the strength of my heart and my portion forever," said the psalmist. "Never will I leave you; never will I forsake you," said our Lord (Heb. 13:5). It's a guarantee that we can count on and live by.

 Forgive me for my many failures, dear Lord. Even if my body grows weaker, may your grace strengthen my spirit. Amen.

Affirm this truth today: "God is the strength of my heart and my portion forever."

■ WHOSE SIDE IS GOD ON?

Psalm 74:   ''Why does your anger smolder against the sheep of your pasture?'' (v. 1).

We wonder at times: whose side is God on? We wonder about it when missionaries are tortured and killed, when thousands of human beings of all ages are massacred, when churches are demolished and faithful Christians are persecuted.

According to the psalmist, these things happen because God is chastening his creatures, taking out his anger over their faithlessness, or just looking the other way when these terrible things are going on. The psalmist seemed to assume that God retained absolute control over everything that happened.

Some people still assume this, though we should know better. In giving his children the freedom to love or hate, to create or destroy, God submitted to the terrible risk of seeing his beloved children suffer. Was this the only way they could become and remain his sons and daughters?

God is on our side, and God's victory is ultimately our victory. In the meantime, God is bearing with us the suffering and pain we are subject to on this earthly journey.

 I can't understand, O God; I can only trust that I am your child and that nothing that happens to me here will endanger that relationship. Amen.

When you are confused by the suffering around you, remind yourself that God is with us and shares our suffering.

■ AN EXCELLENT EXERCISE

Psalm 77: "I will remember the deeds of the Lord" (v. 11).

It is an exercise and discipline we should all participate in: remembering the deeds of the Lord. Our experiences of what God has done for us in the past will better enable us to face life on this world as the days pass before us. He has made known his love to us in uncountable ways. While we may not be aware of all the occasions when divine grace came to our rescue, there are some incidents in which we strongly sensed God's power and presence. There were answers to desperate prayers—for healing, for wisdom to make a correct decision, for deliverance from some threat to our life.

"Has his unfailing love vanished forever? Has his promise failed for all time? Has God forgotten to be merciful?" Don't you believe it! "Jesus Christ is the same yesterday and today and forever" (Heb. 13:8). Others may forget about us or ignore us. The world may no longer have much need for us. Our relationship to God, however, is never endangered, and we are his beloved children forever. "What god is so great as our God?" The answer is in his mighty deeds of our past and his precious promises concerning our future.

 I give thanks unto God, for he is good, and his love endures forever. Amen.

Recall the incidents in your life when you most strongly sensed God's power and presence.

■ SET FREE TO SERVE

Psalm 81:   "I removed the burden from their shoulders; their hands were set free from the basket" (v. 6).

The psalmist could be describing the life of retirement. The burden of nine-to-five, five-days-a-week, labor in the marketplace has been lifted from our shoulders. We are relieved from the heavy responsibilities of family support. This, at least, is the idea and ideal of retirement.

As interpreted through the revelations of the New Testament, however, the words of the psalm writer have a more important meaning. They could be the grand proclamation of the glorious news of our release from sin's guilt and eternal consequences. We have been set free to serve; we are now the children and servants of God.

While the servants of God are commissioned to serve him by serving his children at all times and wherever they are placed, retirement offers the freedom to serve in special ways, unimpeded by the need for remuneration. It is called voluntary service; it could be loving service to others as the ministers of God and disciples of Jesus Christ. Our Lord's command is still to "go, and make disciples." He has given us the gifts and will teach us the ways in which we can do this.

 Teach me, O Master, how to use my time and gifts to carry out your purposes in these years that are left to me. Amen.

In what ways has retirement freed you to serve God and others?

■ WE HAVE WHAT WE NEED

Psalm 84: "No good thing does he withhold from those whose walk is blameless" (v. 11).

The apostle Peter wrote: "His divine power has given us everything we need for life and godliness" (2 Peter 1:3). The New Testament has proved the ancient psalmist was right: no good thing has been held back from God's redeemed children. Through Jesus Christ, our God "has given us his very great and precious promises, so that through them you may participate in the divine nature" (2 Peter 1:4).

Our natural faculties do not enable us to joyfully and productively handle our years of retirement or to prepare us for that new and everlasting life awaiting us. Nonetheless, God makes us capable, not only to *endure* our final years, but to *enjoy* them as his happy and fruitful servants. He has given us his Spirit; he indwells and empowers us. He has set us free to serve and, withholding no good thing from us, has given us whatever is necessary to be his loving, effective servants wherever our journey may take us.

Can you believe it? As older-but-wiser Christians in this conflict-ridden world we are to carry on the incarnation of God. Through our love for others we can communicate God's love and healing to lonely, frightened, broken people around us.

 O Lord, may your love for me be channeled through me to unloved and hurting people around me. Amen.

How can you be a channel for God's love to unloved and hurting people in your community?

■ RESTORATION

Psalm 85:   "Restore us again, O God our Savior"
(v. 4).

We are aware of the joy of restoration. We
remember the new light in our children's eyes when,
after their "crime and punishment," they were
completely restored to our arms and affections. There
are few human experiences as warm as that of our
restoration to the love of our mates after some
senseless spat.

We frequently need restoration to God our Savior.
Our salvation itself is not in question: "For it is by
grace you have been saved, through faith—and this not
from yourselves, it is the gift of God" (Eph. 2:8).
There are times, however, when we need to be
restored to the joy and peace that God grants through
his gift of salvation.

Unfortunately we are dependent on our feelings to
keep us in good spirits. Thank God for good feelings,
but don't rely on them. There are those days when
they fail to show up. The psalmist too was driven to
the "blues," but most of his songs conclude with a
chorus of joy and praise.

God does restore us to himself with reminders of
his love and promises of his eternal presence. The
closer we live to his grace and promises, the brighter
our days will be.

 Forgive my failures and infidelities, O Lord, and
restore to me the joy of my salvation. Amen.

**Think back on times in your life when you
experienced restoration with a family member, a
friend, or with God.**

■ A NEW VOCATION

Psalm 86: "Teach me your way, O Lord, and I will walk in your truth" (v. 11).

Retirement for most of us is not just one long *vacation*; it is a new *vocation*. We are set free to serve in new ways, new churches, new arenas of life. "I chose you to go and bear fruit," said Jesus to his disciples (John 15:16). To "walk in God's truth" is to walk with God; and that means we continue to work for him, to be his servants, whatever our age and wherever we are.

Nothing is so dismal and destructive to the human spirit as life without meaning or purpose. For some of us retirement may be the time for discovering new meaning and purpose for our lives. Such a purpose may be as simple as tending our own little gardens or helping to rear our grandchildren or relating lovingly to our neighbors across the street. This is a vocation— as is learning how to live in solitariness and writing letters to other lonely people.

Really, walking in the truth is our vocation. Retirement simply adds new dimensions, and walking in God's truth for our lives will result in ministering to others in concern and love.

 O God, forgive me for cluttering up my life with self-centered ambitions and keep me focused on your will for my life. Amen.

Now that you're retired, what do you see as your vocation in life?

■ THOSE FINAL YEARS

Psalm 88: "For my soul is full of troubles, and my life draws near the grave" (v. 3).

This is truly a song of despair, a bit like some of our contemporary "blues." Most of us sing the "blues" from time to time. We called it "blue Monday" in preretirement days when we had to face another 40-hour week of hard labor. Most of the troubles that meet us along with the sunrise are small troubles that pester us just enough to take the shine out of the sun and send us mumbling, bumbling through the day.

Our Lord has no objection to our sharing them with him. It might be good for us to sing our "blues" to God. Our final years may be a bit brighter, however, if we take each day as a shiny new gift from him. It is sad to needlessly waste any of our days as our lives draw "near to the grave."

God alone can wipe away the tears of those seasons of deep despair that may increase as we approach the end of the journey. Even if the fear of dying no longer disturbs us, there is no sorrow as painful as the loss of a mate, a son or daughter, even a dear friend. But if our lives are immersed in the love of God, his grace will eventually come through as strength and comfort to us.

Gracious God, I gratefully accept the day before me as a new opportunity, a new experience and adventure. May you be glorified in me this day. Amen.

Memorize today's prayer and use it to begin each day.

■ GO WITH GOD

Psalm 89: "Blessed are those . . . who walk in the light of your presence, O Lord" (v. 15).

The psalmist was not promising that everything will always be sweet and lovely for those who walk in the light of God's presence. Even as he sang about all the blessings that will follow and shelter David, the chosen one, the psalmist interjected a negative note: "What man can live and not see death? . . . O Lord, where is your former great love, which in your faithfulness you swore to David?"

The path before us will not be without its ominous shadows. There will be fears and doubts, obstacles to surmount, pains to endure, problems to solve. There will be frustrations and discouragements to hamper us. Serenity will be an inner strength that calms and supports us as we struggle and sometimes stumble along.

Despite the traumatic realities of aging, there is a far greater reality that diminishes and softens the anguish of these lesser realities. We who walk in the light of God's presence, trusting in his promises, embracing and reflecting his love, may walk with a light step even when our bodies are heavy with age and illness. The grace and energy of God will go with us, for we are the "blessed" of the Lord.

 Whether it be shadows or sunshine, O Lord, I claim your grace to walk courageously and devotedly as your child and servant. Amen.

Read the little classic, "Practicing the Presence of God" by Brother Lawrence.

■ SELF-PITY

Psalm 90: "The length of our days is seventy years—or eighty if we have the strength; yet their span is but trouble and sorrow, for they quickly pass, and we fly away" (v. 10).

The psalmist obviously felt sorry for himself in this psalm and, since he lacked revelations available to 20th-century Christians, he succeeds in evoking our sympathy.

Sometimes we experience self-pity too. While aging is supposed to be a rich and fruitful experience, offering us the opportunity to shed our preretirement anxieties, to relax and to do the things we had no time for in our working years, it does not turn out that way for many of us. So much of our life has passed quickly by, and we worry about the rest. Focusing negatively on this final period of our lives often gives rise to self-pity.

Today is today. It may be the last day of our lives, our final time on this earth to laugh and play or complete some unfinished task, right a wrong, fulfill an obligation, or to touch someone with love. It would be a shame to waste it on self-pity.

 Thank you for this day, O Lord; it is truly a precious gift. Grant that I may use it to glorify you. Amen.

Determine today to resist any temptations to self-pity. Ask God to help you live positively.

■ SALVATION AMID SUFFERING

Psalm 91: "I will be with him in trouble, I will deliver him and honor him . . . and show him my salvation" (v. 15-16).

The psalmist was a bit impetuous in these beautiful declarations and promises concerning God's care for his children. While we are most certainly surrounded by God's love and secure in his promise of eternal life, the experience of past saints as well as our own throws into question many of the psalmist's proclamations concerning the "terror of the night . . . the arrow that flies by day . . . the pestilence that stalks in darkness." Evil does befall us; scourges do come near our tents; and angels do not always keep us from dashing our feet against stones.

Jesus makes no such promises. He prophesies persecution. He predicts that all who follow him will suffer, and some will die for the sake of God's kingdom. Our Lord commands us to take up our cross and follow him (Mark 8:34). Someone has stated that "to go with the cross on your shoulder is to have already received the death sentence."

Sometimes it is hard for us to reconcile God's care with the plight of many who trust and worship him. Still we can rest in the psalmist's assurance that God will be with us in trouble and will deliver and honor us and show us his salvation.

 I thank you, O God, that even the suffering that befalls me can serve your purposes in my life. Amen.

Several times today repeat the thought, "God is with me in trouble. He will deliver me and show me his salvation."

■ HALLELUJAH!

Psalm 92: "They will still bear fruit in old age, they will stay fresh and green" (v. 14).

This is a psalm that should make our day. It may not be particularly flattering to be considered "fresh and green," but it signifies life and energy and fruitfulness, despite wrinkles and aching joints and old-fashioned ideas. We really can celebrate our postretirement vocation. We will not shake up the world or make headlines, but we can "still bear fruit in old age."

It is this, after all, that counts with God—probably far more than some of your young and middle-age achievements that are now memories. Having matured and mellowed through our many years, we can exhibit the fruit of the Spirit, which, according to the apostle Paul, is "love, joy, peace, patience, kindness, goodness, faithfulness, gentleness, self-control" (Gal. 5:22).

This will give purpose to our years. Our real vocation, by God's choice and commission, is being God's servants to others. Even as we busy our hands with lawns and gardens, or some other artistic enterprise or hobby, we can "bring forth fruit in old age."

 O Lord, may I never forget that your call to salvation is also a call to servanthood. Amen.

In what ways do you still hope to "bear fruit" in old age? Ask God to help you do this.

■ THE PAIN OF MATURATION

Psalm 94: "Blessed is the man you discipline,
O Lord" (v. 12).

While most of the pain so rampant in our world
today is caused by God's human creatures hurting one
another, there is the problem of pain which is not our
direct responsibility. The psalmist posed the problem
and accepted many of the terrible things that befell
him and his people as a discipline that served to
purify God's children and prepare them for God-
centered worship and service.

We cannot hold God responsible for the painful
things that happen to us. We can, however, find the
Christian answer to suffering. It is to face it, accept it,
and use it. We cannot escape suffering any more than
we can be totally unselfish or sinless. We can,
however, accept it as a discipline that will strengthen
our faith and mature us as the children and
servants of God.

"We also rejoice in our sufferings," wrote the
apostle Paul, "because we know that suffering
produces perseverance" (Rom. 5:3).

 Loving God, enable me to grow and mature as
your child and servant even in the midst of my
conflicts and pains. Amen.

**Write a prayer asking God to help you face suffering,
accept it, and use it.**

■ JOYFUL SONGS

Psalm 95: "Come, let us sing for joy to the Lord" (v. 1).

The success or failure of each day is often dependent on how we greet the sunrise—or the inclement weather that may be closing in on us. All too often the sounds we make as we climb out of our warm nests are anything but joyful. They extend all the way from grumbling over aching backs to negative remarks, and we have nothing but contempt for the TV-commercial personality who rises with a beaming smile and a joyous exclamation over a particular brand of breakfast food awaiting her. That negative response sometimes sets the pattern for another wasted day, and reading a psalm or a meditation like this one may not make a smidgen of difference.

It doesn't have to be that way. The psalmist encourages us to "sing for joy to the Lord." In many of his psalms he gives us reasons for that kind of greeting to any day. After all, it's another day, another gift, another opportunity, another adventure.

Finding reasons for joyful songs may involve considerable discipline, but it is worth the effort. The best reason of all, of course, is that Jesus died for our sins and rose again to grant us everlasting life. "Come, let us sing for joy to the Lord!"

 O Lord, I come before you with thanksgiving. May this day be filled with joyful exclamations and songs of praise. Amen.

Find a song of joy you can read or sing to greet each day.

■ CHANGING OUR TUNE

Psalm 98: "Sing to the Lord a new song" (v. 1).

A new vocation or a new milestone in life, such as retirement, ought to inspire new songs. When in our youth we came to the place of consciously embracing God's amazing grace for our lives, we changed our tunes and began to sing new songs. They may have been some of the old hymns that can never be replaced, but they suddenly became new and precious to us. While the world sings lustily before the altars of sensualism, materialism, nationalism, or shallow concepts of love and life, the children of God change their tunes along with their life-styles and sing the new and yet ancient songs that celebrate the "marvelous things" that God has done.

Whether we sing, play guitars, or blow trumpets, the sound of happy and worshipful melodies can emerge from our lives. We will not be able to drown out the noises of the world, the cries of hunger, the fears of nuclear annihilation, the raucous shrieks of cheap thrills in entertainment centers, or the mournful "blues" of sad and lonely people, but we can inject into it all the major chords of hope and genuine joy and divine love.

Whatever we do, let's keep singing and making joyful songs. Let us fill our lives and homes and sanctuaries with the sounds of celebration!

 "Oh, for a thousand tongues to sing my great Redeemer's praise, the glories of my God and King, the triumphs of his grace!" Amen.

How can you use music to add more joy to your life?

■ GRACE AND JUDGMENT

Psalm 99: "The Lord reigns; let the nations tremble" (v. 1).

There is trembling and trepidation in an honest and sincere approach to God. He is not "the man upstairs" or some benign grandfather that people sometimes make him out to be. He is God. "Let the nations tremble! . . . Let them praise your great and awesome name . . . he is holy." The psalmist could not have known God as we do through his Son, Jesus Christ, but he knew and understood enough to solemnly respect him. And he did this despite the heathen about him who ridiculed his God.

While the nations may need to tremble in fear because he is a God of judgment and will hold the faithless and disobedient accountable for their selfish deeds, the redeemed will tremble in respectful but joyous ecstasy because he is a God of grace who saves and honors those who embrace him and communicate his eternal love to their fellow creatures about them.

We may be tempted, in our carelessness, to treat him as just another factor in our lives or reduce him to some Sunday-morning caper in our affairs. Instead, it is good to frequently contemplate the awesomeness of God. "Exalt the Lord our God . . . for the Lord our God is holy." The Lord reigns.

 You are not my servant, O God; I am yours. I pray that you will always reign supreme in my heart, my life, and all my activities. Amen.

Read the book by J. B. Phillips, *Your God Is Too Small.*

■ REASON FOR SELF-ESTEEM

Psalm 100: "We are his people, the sheep of his pasture" (v. 3).

We have good reason to rejoice, to "serve the Lord with gladness" and "come before him with joyful songs." We can rejoice because we know that "the Lord is God" and "we are his people, the sheep of his pasture."

This gives us good reason for self-esteem. A famous preacher insists that "at the deepest level, all social, political, economic, religious, and even scientific problems relate to the private and collective need for positive pride, or healthy self-esteem." Whereas we may have had some satisfying successes in our younger years that contributed to our feelings of self-worth, we may feel otherwise now that we are retired from the world's workforce and considered by many to be spent, wasted, and about to be retired from life itself.

It is time we learn that our worth or esteem is not determined by past successes or our visible contributions to society. It was predetermined by God himself and is always in effect. "We are his people, the sheep of his pasture." There is no one who can be more significant and no way in which we can be more esteemed than that.

 I rejoice, my great God, that you have through Jesus Christ made me worthy as your child and servant. Amen.

Strengthen your self-esteem by reminding yourself that you are God's child and ambassador.

■ AS THE DAYS PASS BY

Psalm 102:   "For my days vanish like smoke" (v. 3).

In this psalm we hear the cry of despondency over the swiftly passing days of aging and the loneliness that often accompanies those days.

There will be days like this for most of us despite our firm claim on self-worth and self-esteem. Life in this dimension is indeed fragile and finite; the days we spend on this globe are relatively few. The assurance of life after death was not as secure or indisputable for the psalmist as it is for those of us who follow the resurrected Christ. Yet we also may "feel like a bird alone on a housetop."

We will not be able to totally block out such feelings and must therefore learn how to deal with them. The psalmist attempted to do this by affirming what he really was convinced about. He said to God, "You remain the same, and your years will never end." Having strayed from the main road on our own little side-trips on obscure paths that lead only to doubt and despair, we must turn back to the well-marked highway and affirm our faith and rediscover our joy in our God who is "enthroned forever."

My days vanish like smoke, O Lord, but not your love or my security therein. May my faith become stronger and my witness more positive and emphatic as the days go by. Amen.

When you feel like "a bird alone on a housetop," say to God, "You remain the same, and your years will never end."

■ HOW TO FEEL YOUNGER

Psalm 103: "Praise the Lord, O my soul; and forget not all his benefits" (v. 2).

Would you like to feel a bit younger? Then read this magnificent psalm aloud—and with gusto! Relish for a few moments those exhilarating words: "forgives . . . heals . . . redeems . . . crowns . . . satisfies." The psalmist claims that this is youth-renewing, and it is, even if our wrinkles don't vanish and our aches won't go away.

The psalmist was aware of a man's finitude: "his days are like grass, he flourishes like a flower of the field; the wind blows over it, and it is gone." But he also knew that "from everlasting to everlasting the Lord's love is with those who fear him." If St. Francis preached to the birds, we can broadcast this to whatever or whomever is within earshot of this fabulous truth. Shout it out!

Now don't you feel a little younger? Read it again: "For as high as the heavens are above the earth, so great is his love for those who fear him; as far as the east is from the west, so far has he removed our transgressions from us."

It is the blessed gospel of God's grace—to be believed and proclaimed. Remarkably and beautifully expressed by the psalmist, it has been explicitly revealed to us through Jesus Christ. We are young forever.

 "Praise the Lord, O my soul; all my inmost being, praise his holy name." Amen.

Look for an opportunity to share this marvelous psalm.

■ HOW GREAT IS OUR GOD!

Psalm 104: "O Lord my God, you are very great!
. . . How many are your works, O Lord" (vv. 1, 24).

It is impossible to describe God or to picture the
One who is not confined to our three-dimensional
planet. Yet the psalmist uses every similitude and
metaphor he can think of to sing about the greatness
of his God. In this psalm he focuses on the greatness
of God as revealed in the creation of the world and its
creatures. In Psalm 105 he proclaims God's greatness
and glory as manifested in his dealings with his human
creatures—particularly the children of Israel.
"Remember the wonders he has done, his miracles,
and the judgments he pronounced," wrote the
psalmist.

How great is our God! The words of Psalm 139
express the frustration as well as the utter impossibility
of measuring or imagining that greatness: "Such
knowledge is too wonderful for me, too lofty for me to
attain" (v. 6). In the midst of a nuclear threat, the
economic failures, the starving millions, and our own
conflicts and weaknesses, we need to be assured of the
greatness of our God.

Our God is truly great, and wherever his creatures
yield their lives into his hands and are indwelt and
motivated by his grace and power, that greatness is
revealed.

You have kept me through the difficult past, O
Lord; you will walk with me into the perilous
future. I thank and praise you for your love.
Amen.

Try writing your own psalm of praise to God.

■ FROM GRUMBLE TO GRATITUDE

Psalm 106: "They grumbled in their tents, and did not obey the Lord" (v. 25).

The psalmist described what happened to his people as they took their long journey through the wilderness. The joy of their great deliverance from the armies of Pharoah faded out during the many trials and difficulties of their journey. The days became boring, the daily chores tedious, the miracles of their great God were few and far between. "They soon forgot what he had done and did not wait for his counsel . . . they forgot the God who saved them. . . . They grumbled in their tents."

It is not an unusual picture of the unfaithfulness of God's children. We recognize it in our own hearts and affairs. Grumbling did not begin with the Israelites— nor did it end there. The ecstasy that accompanied our early consciousness of God's love and our great deliverance from sin into salvation is now hard to come by. Miracles are few and far between. Instead of soaring through the heavens we are stumbling along dusty, rock-strewn paths. Sometimes we grumble in our tents.

Our gracious, patient, loving God understands. He bids us to remember what he has done for us, and to faithfully and obediently plod along despite the present tedium and boredom. There will be ecstasy enough for all of us at the end of our journey.

 Give thanks to the Lord, for he is good; his love endures for ever. Amen.

When you're tempted to grumble, focus on expressing gratitude for what God has done and is still doing for you.

■ EFFECTIVE EVANGELISM

Psalm 107:   "Let the redeemed of the Lord say so" (v. 2 RSV).

Amazing as it may seem in our sophisticated culture with all of its gimmicks and gadgets, programs, surveys, and clever subtle ways of maneuvering and manipulating the masses, the most effectual evangelism is stated by the psalmist and demonstrated by Jesus Christ in very simple words: "Let the redeemed of the Lord say so." Without putting down mass evangelistic campaigns and the entertaining programs of the electronic church, we need to be reminded that the oldest method of evangelism is still the most effective. It is the personal witness and testimony of each of us concerning God's forgiving, redeeming, everlasting love as revealed through Jesus Christ.

It is not our task to convert people to Christ; that must be done by the Holy Spirit. Our assignment is to reveal God and his love to people about us, and this is done by relating to them, listening to them, loving them, responding to their needs wherever possible, sharing ourselves with them, and when the proper moment arrives, to proclaim or witness to the redeeming and healing power of God.

We who love the Lord are already equipped to do just this—right where we are, with people we meet and befriend. This is an important part of our new vocation.

 Grant to me, O Lord, the courage and opportunities to involve myself lovingly in the lives and needs of others and thereby to witness to your saving love. Amen.

Think of one person near you to whom you would like to witness. Look for an opportunity to do so.

■ WHEN ONE IS WISE

Psalm 111: "The fear of the Lord is the beginning of wisdom" (v. 10).

Most of us would agree, no doubt, that the wisest thing we ever did in and with our lives was to yield them to the love and ownership of God. We were created by God and for God. We are incomplete apart from God. We are able to find true and eternal joy only in God.

We have vacillated; we have compromised; we have been unfaithful servants. We have had our doubts and fears, our ups and downs. We have been attracted by the world's glitter and tempted by its siren songs. We have even succumbed to some of its seductive passions. We did not, however, find real meaning and purpose for our lives until we were drawn back into God's orbit and reinstated in his plan and purpose for us.

Is it possible that someone who reads this has still not discovered the wisdom of yielding to and walking in God's will for his or her life? It is still not too late. God's grace is always sufficient and available to those who will turn to him. "Come to me, all you who are weary and burdened, and I will give you rest. Take my yoke upon you and learn from me" (Matt. 11:28-29). It will be the wisest thing you have ever done.

 Gracious Father, even when I failed you, you have never failed me. I give thanks to you with all my heart. Amen.

Today, by a definite act of will, commit, or recommit your life to God and his purposes.

■ GOD'S CHILD IN A BAD-NEWS WORLD

Psalm 112: "He will have no fear of bad news"
(v. 7).

Bad news is not peculiar to our day. It began in the Garden of Eden. Whereas it often took months to receive news back in ancient history, we now hear and see bad news even as it happens throughout our world. We are oversaturated with bad news.

The psalm writer is not implying that the one who trusts the Lord is in any way shielded from the bad news, but he states that "his heart is secure, he will have no fear." Before we tune in on radio and TV news programs each morning, it might be wise to tune in on God. This will not block out bad news, but it will firm up our faith and allay our fears about the obscene, ugly happenings that assault us each day.

Even as we praise God and grow in our faith and find solace in him despite bad news, we realize that the terrible things that happen throughout our world are also happening to our sisters and brothers, and our praise is interspersed with pain and sorrow on their behalf. We may control our fears; we must share their suffering by interceding and acting on their behalf.

 O God, be very near to your children who are suffering today. In their hours of pain, enable them to sense your presence and power. Amen.

When you hear bad news on television or radio, offer a quick prayer for the people involved.

■ WE ARE SERVANTS

Psalm 113: "Praise, O servants of the Lord, praise the name of the Lord" (v. 1).

There is really no such thing as retirement for the children of God. Even if health fails or arthritis cripples or the reflexes fail to respond as they used to, we are servants of God. This means not only do we continue to "praise the name of the Lord" and always give "thanks to God for everything" (Eph. 5:20), but that we serve him, for we are his servants forever.

Retirement does not signal the end of all things for Christians, but new vocations, new places, a new set of conditions, a new arena in which to carry out our servanthood. We can be Christ's servants and serve him whatever our condition and wherever we are. We can even serve him through suffering or in solitude or from a bed of pain and apparent helplessness.

Our Lord "raises the poor from the dust and lifts the needy from the ash heap." He does this and most other deeds of grace and mercy through his servants, who are his hands and feet committed to carrying out his purposes and channeling his love and healing to broken people about them.

 I do praise you, great God, and seek from you the grace and strength I need to keep serving you. Amen.

Ask God to show you how you can be his servant in your present situation.

■ NO OTHER GODS

Psalm 115: "Not to us, O Lord, not to us but to your name be the glory" (v. 1).

One of the advantages of aging is that we have been able to cast off many of the idols we have accumulated throughout our younger years. We are not likely to kowtow to any guru that appears on the scene and captivates the imaginations of naive young people. Whereas some of our peers are still led astray by the charlatans and con artists that play on the spiritual needs of their victims, most of us, like the prodigal son of Christ's parable, have come to our senses and returned to God and his purposes for our lives.

Yet there may still be loopholes in our lives that need plugging up, malignant infections within our spirits that need purging. It is possible to give glory to the wrong things, and our dependence on such things could be as idolatrous as were the activities of the heathen in the day of the psalm writer.

It is for this reason that we need the discipline as well as the desire to return continually to the Source of all life, love, and joy, to give glory to the only true God and to commit ourselves to praising and serving him.

 Forgive, O Lord, my inordinate affections for the things of this world. Restore and increase my love and adoration for you. Amen.

Stop and think: Are there any idols in your life that prevent you from glorifying God above all things?

■ KEEPING THE LINES OPEN

Psalm 116:   "I will call on him as long as I live"
(v. 2).

The psalmist's hope was kept alive by his continual communication with God. He kept the lines open between him and his Creator. He determined, "I will call on him as long as I live." This does not mean that the psalmist was then able to "think God" every minute of every day. Nevertheless, God was his North Star, his guide. No one and nothing was as important to him as God: "I love the Lord, for he heard my voice; he heard my cry for mercy."

We have been redeemed and reconciled to God through Jesus Christ, who extinguished our fear of death with his promise of eternal life. Because he is our supreme hope in this final stage of our earthly sojourn, we can keep our lines open to God's voice and our lives in loving subordination to his will and purposes.

This is done through praises, prayers, and meditation. We will hear him speak to us through the Scriptures and sense his embracing touch by way of the Lord's Supper. We walk in obedience before him in our loving service to our fellow persons on his behalf.

 I praise and adore you, my loving God, because you continue to hear my voice and my supplications. Amen.

Make this your aim: "I will call upon God as long as I live."

■ EVERY DAY IS A GIFT

Psalm 118: "This is the day which the Lord has made; let us rejoice and be glad in it" (v. 24).

Perhaps you have heard a pastor make this verse from the psalms a call to worship at a church service. Even if that pastor said nothing else, it would be a "sermon" worth remembering. The psalmist's proclamation ought to be especially meaningful for those of us who are retired.

Every day is indeed a gift, one more day to be with our grandchildren or tend our gardens, to walk through the woods, to watch the sun rise, to be reconciled to those we have hurt, demonstrate our love to those about us, to write a letter or listen to a symphony. The Lord made this day for us, and, according to the psalmist, it is a day in which to "rejoice and be glad."

Who is the psalmist trying to fool? There are days when neither he nor his readers are inclined to "rejoice and be glad." There is "a time to weep, and a time to laugh, a time to mourn and a time to dance" (Eccl. 3:4). Surely the psalmist's recommendation cannot include every day.

Maybe not, but there is nothing to lose in making the attempt—to use the gift of each day as a time for turning unto God and finding, in spite of clouds and shadows, a reason for joy and gladness.

 You are, O Lord, my strength and my song as well as my salvation. I sing your praises and seek to serve your purposes on this day that you have made for me. Amen.

Begin each day with this determination: "This is the day which the Lord has made; I will rejoice and be glad in it."

■ JUST PASSING THROUGH

Psalm 119:1-25:   "I am a stranger on earth" (v. 19).

A few days before her death, the writer Clare McCarthy penned this eloquent testimony: "When the time of our particular sunset comes, our thing, our accomplishment won't really matter a great deal. But the clarity and care with which we have loved others will speak with vitality of the great gift of life we have been for each other."

Many human beings live out their earthbound existence as if it were a self-centered, one-track journey that leads nowhere. By contrast, the psalmist dedicated his life's sojourn to God as revealed to him through his laws. He was also limited in his outlook, but faithfully endeavored to live according to that which he had been taught. The Christian, on the other hand, understands his life as a journey within God's orbit of grace in which his life becomes a vehicle of God's love to others along the way.

"A new commandment I give you. . . . As I have loved you, so you must love one another," said Jesus (John 13:34). If any of our contributions to this world account for anything at all, it will be those contributions of love that we have expended on one another during our short sojourn on this planet.

 You have given me life through your love, O God. Enable me to share that life in my love for others. Amen.

Copy out the quote from Clare McCarthy. Tape it where you can see it each day.

■ WHEN WE NEED HELP

Psalm 121: "He who watches over you will not slumber" (v. 3).

Some of us may pride ourselves in being relatively self-reliant through our youthful and middle-age years. There are few of us who will proceed very many years beyond retirement without receiving some help or assistance along the way. We seek financial help from government and insurance companies, or medical assistance from hospitals and clinics, and the time may come when we have to turn to our children or community-care agencies for help of one kind or another.

Whereas our help comes from the Lord, it comes through agencies and individuals who are God's servants carrying out his purposes. The Lord, our keeper, does not sleep, but some of us as his servants, and even some churches, are sleeping on the job in respect to being God's channels of loving service to those who need help in our communities.

Our great God helps us even as we help one another. When we are no longer able to serve, he serves us through the concern and love of able people about us. Truly, "He who watches over you will not slumber."

 Awaken me, dear Lord, to the needs of people about me that I can serve, and may I thankfully and unashamedly accept their gifts of love when I am no longer able to serve. Amen.

Ask God each day to lead you to those who need your help and those who can help you.

■ FREE AT LAST

Psalm 124: "The snare has been broken, and we have escaped" (v. 7).

If the Lord had not been on our side," we would never have made it to retirement; we would not have been delivered from the eternal consequences of our sin; we would have no hope for life beyond death, we could look forward to no happiness other than that which we sought for in the transitory things of this life; we would probably have been enslaved and possibly destroyed by the forces of evil, if not by our own selfishness and greed; we would have missed out on the most beautiful experiences of life and would never have discovered our real purpose for being on this world.

We are reading this psalm and meditation today because the Lord was and is on our side. Our snare, also, "has been broken, and we have escaped." It was broken when Jesus went to the cross on our behalf. The bonds of sin, the chains of death, the fires of hell, have been vanquished once and for all by way of the death and resurrection of Jesus Christ.

Let us fill our sanctuaries, our homes, the woods and hills, streets and shopping malls, with sounds of praise and thanksgiving. We have escaped! We are free from sin's curse to serve God forever. Let us rejoice!

 I have by your grace, O Lord, escaped from the "fowler's snare." May my life be a perpetual offering of thanksgiving to you. Amen.

Let this be your guiding thought today: "The Lord is on my side."

■ SURROUNDED BY CONCERN

Psalm 125: "As the mountains surround Jerusalem, so the Lord surrounds his people" (v. 2).

We might wonder just how it was possible for the psalmist to be so assured of God's concern for and protection of his chosen people. It may have been the great stories that had come down to him—the miraculous deliverance from Egypt, the receiving of the law at Mount Sinai, and other events in which God showed his hand and spoke through his prophets. It was obvious to the psalmist that the children of Abraham were indeed the children of God.

Jerusalem, however, was often plundered and ravished by Israel's enemies, despite the mountains that surrounded that great city. So were the faithful among the chosen people of God, despite the psalmist's conviction that this great God would watch over and protect them and surround them with his love like the mountains round about Jerusalem. The sorrows and adversities that have befallen the children of Israel throughout the centuries are almost beyond description.

We will find little comfort in this song and analogy of the psalmist if we assume that God's surrounding will make us immune to the pain and suffering, the conflicts and defeats, frustrations and aggravations that afflict all of us at times. Our comfort is in the fact that even in the midst of these negatives in life, we truly are surrounded by God's concern and love and are secure in our relationship to him.

 I thank you, dear God, that within the storms that sweep in on me, my relationship to you is forever. Amen.

Find a picture of mountains. Make a poster using today's Bible verse.

■ TIME FOR HILARITY

Psalm 126: "Those who sow in tears will reap with songs of joy" (v. 5).

How do we know we are growing older? "Our children begin to look middle-aged. Our knees buckle but our belts won't. We have all the answers, but nobody asks us the right questions. That gleam in our eyes is really the sun reflected off our trifocals. Our backs go out more than we do. People are beginning to address us as 'old-timers.'"

At least one of the reasons for aging is the tears we have sown throughout the years. There have been both good and sad times. There will be more to come. In spite of those arthritic twings, however, we can be happier than we have ever been. Life has been full of dark nights, but we now see the light at the end of the tunnel. It is time to celebrate. We ought to acknowledge our Lord's love and concern, our secure and eternal relationship to him, and allow our bodies and spirits to break forth into happy hilarity and give our nerves and muscles the healthy exercise of laughter.

We are now on the "reaping" end of our lives. We may not have many sheaves to bring with us or accomplishments to brag about, but God knows what we have done for him in this life. He accepts us as we are and bids us fill "our mouths . . . with laughter and our tongues with songs of joy."

 My sojourn through the aging process is my coming home to you, my God. I am grateful and I am glad. Amen.

Spend a few minutes today contemplating the joys of going home to God.

■ LETTING GO AND LETTING GOD

Psalms 127-128:   "In vain you rise early and stay up late, toiling for food to eat" (127:2).

Some of the regrets we have concerning our pre-retirement years have to do with those times in which we have labored in vain, attempting in the strength of our own egos and knowledge to do those things and carry out those projects that only God can do. Instead of allowing him to carry out his projects through us, we often played god and worked only for personal gain; or we simply assumed that our projects were God's projects. It resulted in early rising, staying up late, and bouts with insomnia.

All this is in the past for most of us. While not all of our children are "like olive shoots" around our table, some of them, in spite of or partly because of us, give us pride and joy. When we arrived at the point where we ceased shepherding them and committed them to our God as their Creator and Savior, we realized our anxiety had been in vain.

It continues to be much the same with all the other projects that we have tangled with throughout our lives. While we remain concerned about them, the time for early risings, late nights, and debilitating anxieties is over. Let us accept God's blessing as those "who fear the Lord, who walk in his ways."

 I commit into your hands, O Lord, my home, children, and grandchildren, and all my past projects and concerns. Help me now to be happy and faithful as I walk in your paths. Amen.

Identify the concerns of life over which you are still anxious. Commit them to God this day.

◼ WE ARE FORGIVEN

Psalm 130: "If you kept a record of sins, O Lord, who could stand?" (v. 3).

At times the failures or defeats of our past years will hit us like a ton of bricks. While God forgives and forgets, how difficult for us to do either! We may have never really forgiven ourselves for some of the things that have happened because of our weaknesses and indiscretions. It isn't likely that we will ever forget about them.

The song of the psalmist registers both a comforting and a searing question: "If you kept a record of sins, O Lord, who could stand?" The answer follows: "But with you there is forgiveness." Speaking from personal experience the apostle John declared, "If we confess our sins, he is faithful and just and will forgive us our sins and purify us from all unrighteousness" (1 John 1:9). Our sins—past, present, and future—were removed in that amazing act of God back there on Calvary's hill when Jesus died for the sins of all humankind.

The psalmist had to look to personal insight and prophetic proclamations for his assurance of forgiveness; we need only return to Christ's cross and there claim anew the forgiving grace and love of God. God help us to leave our burdens at the cross and go on to thanksgiving and celebration.

 I lay my sins on you, Jesus, the spotless Lamb of God; you bear them all and free me from the accurséd load. Amen.

Memorize 1 John 1:9. Repeat it when you need assurance of forgiveness.

■ THE NEED TO RELAX

Psalm 131:   "But I have stilled and quieted my
soul" (v. 2).

What a picture of the golden years! This is what
retirement ought to be about: no races to run, no
competitors to worry about, no prizes to win or
deadlines to meet, no ambitions to satisfy. Is it
possible to live this kind of life? Unless we are
confined to rocking chairs—with our greatest challenge
being in finding the strength to make them go—it
may be neither possible nor wise to expect this of
retirement. It would be boring—if not downright
debilitating.

   Yet the psalmist's beautiful words express well his
relationship of faith and confidence in a loving God.
It could be a description of our relationship to the
psalmist's God, a relationship free from the strain and
stress of struggle or anxiety. We don't have to work
for medals or stars for our crowns. There is nothing
to merit or earn. We need only do what Jesus told
his disciples: "Remain in me, and I will remain in
you . . . that my joy may be in you, and that your
joy may be complete" (John 15:4, 11). We don't have
to be successful, only faithful. He created us,
redeemed us, gifted us with his righteousness. We
are his forever. Let us relax and enjoy it.

 Gracious Father, I am your child forever. I
have need for nothing else. I desire only that
you have your way with me. Amen.

Take time each day to be still and quiet your soul.

■ GROWING OLD TOGETHER

Psalm 133: "How good and pleasant it is when brothers live together in unity!" (v. 1).

The psalmist may not have been as concerned about husband-wife relationships as he was with his relationship to his brothers in the family of Israel. It is, however, of vital concern to those of us who are fortunate enough to still have our marriage partners in these retirement years. It's a new way of life for some of us. Preretirement years often found us going our separate ways. Now we are dealing with a close encounter—so close, in fact, as to cause surprising problems. We discover that the marriage relationship we neglected to work on in previous years must now be realistically dealt with. It can be a delightful experience—discovering each other all over again. But it can also be hectic, even traumatic.

It must be of primary importance and may take all the wisdom of our years to find the goodness and pleasantry of dwelling in unity. We will need God's grace: to respect the other's significance and individuality, to give one another a long leash, to allow the other ample periods of solitude, to come together for frequent periods of mutual prayer and worship, to love each other uncritically and unselfishly. Marriage continues to require conscientious efforts and self-sacrifices; it is worth it when it results in loving unity.

 I thank you, dear God, for my life partner. May your love for us be manifest in our day-by-day relationship to one another. Amen.

Apply the ideas in this devotion to your marriage or other important relationship.

■ IN EVERYTHING GIVE THANKS

Psalm 136:   "Give thanks to the Lord, for he is good. His love endures forever" (v. 1).

Some of us use the first verse of this psalm as a table prayer, but we may not pray it with the emotion and enthusiasm with which the psalmist sang it. He is full of praise and gratitude as he offers thanksgiving for almost everything he can see or hear or remember, in nature about him and in the history of God's merciful dealings with his people.

The psalm writers did not always feel as positive and wholesome about their relationship to God as this psalm indicates. They candidly expressed feelings of doubt and dejection, even accusing God of ignoring them or turning the other way when their enemies threatened them. Yet, despite their frequent negative thoughts about their God, the tone and message of the Psalms are overwhelmingly positive; and they focus on praise and thanksgiving to their God whose "love endures forever."

One of the lessons these psalms teach us is that if we acquire the habit of giving thanks to God for everything around us as well as his merciful dealings with us up to this present time, our faith will be kept fresh and vital. This does not mean that we are thankful for the evil things that happen to us; they are not of God's doing. We give thanks because "his love endures forever."

 Thank you, Lord, for choosing me to be one of your people and for the assurance that your love is forever. Amen.

Throughout this week make a special effort to give thanks to God and to other people.

■ MEANING IN MISERY

Psalm 138: ''Though I walk in the midst of trouble, you preserve my life'' (v.7).

In the many years we have lived, we have discovered that the most destructive suffering is pain without purpose or misery without meaning. We can endure the discomfort of dental work or recovery-room miseries after an operation because there is some purpose behind it. As we age we begin to feel that "everything hurts and what doesn't hurt doesn't work," but even that type of suffering is understandable; portions of our anatomy are simply wearing out and will ultimately give up. Suffering becomes critical when there is no logical reason for it, such as appalling accidents that befall us or our loved ones, or the destruction of God's children through disease or deformities, natural disasters or human violence.

The psalmist found no logical reason in the troubles that beset him, but discovered that in them or despite them, "the Lord will fulfill his purpose for me." "Your love, O Lord, endures forever," repeats the psalmist in an old refrain. What he says to us is that while one may never see any meaning in his misery, the love of God is within that misery. Our comfort and joy is in the fact that "the Lord will fulfill his purpose" for us. We pray, as well, that he will graciously enable us to bear the misery.

 I give thanks to you, dear Lord, that you, too, feel my pain and are ever present to help me bear it and that it will not obstruct your purposes in my life. Amen.

Affirm today: "The Lord will fulfill his purpose for me."

◼ NO PLACE TO HIDE

Psalm 139:1-18: ''You hem me in—behind and before; you have laid your hand upon me'' (v. 5).

It is comforting, though sometimes disconcerting, to realize that there is no place where God is not. He is behind us, before us, above us, and below us, all around us, and still within us. And he is all this not only in his concern and care for us, but also in his loving claim upon us. "You are not your own," wrote Paul. "You were bought at a price. Therefore honor God with your body" (1 Cor. 6:19-20).

No matter how lonely we are in our present circumstances, we are not alone. There is no place in which we can be alone. Our loving God is with us. He has been with us in the past and has already occupied the places and positions we will inhabit in the future. While this ought to give us great joy and comfort, it also lays on us a great responsibility. We are his for his purposes, and we are expected, empowered, and privileged to carry out these purposes wherever we are. We are to reflect and radiate his love, to emulate his concern, and to bear witness to his salvation in our relationships with those who may cross our paths. And God will give us the grace to do so.

 Search me, O God, and know my heart. Test me and know my thoughts. Lead me into joy and ministry as your child and servant. Amen.

Remind yourself often: "I am not alone. God is with me."

■ WHEN WE TALK OUT OF TURN

Psalm 141: "Set a guard over my mouth, O Lord; keep watch over the door of my lips" (v. 3).

It could be one of the benefits of aging—the tendency to talk less, to be less critical of others, to choose our words more carefully, to be more constructive than destructive. It may be because of the blunders of the past or the mellowing that accompanies aging. The times of rash decisions and vehement pronouncements, our assumed need to be dominant or superior over others during the competitive years of youth—these have passed, and we may be more lambs than lions and hopefully a little wiser.

Not all of us are so meek; there are some among us who carry a torch for one thing or another. We ought, however, to be more discerning about the causes we promote and more loving toward our antagonists who can't see things our way. We have discovered by now that God also uses the ministry of others, and thereby reaches people we cannot reach, even though we thought their methods were questionable.

"Consider what a great forest is set on fire by a small spark. The tongue also is a fire," wrote James (3:5-6). Now is the time to think more and talk less. We may then be better enabled to put out some of the fires that rage about us and help to bring unity to the body of Christ.

 Heal those I have hurt through unguarded lips, O Lord, and heal the sickness in my heart that forced my foolish tongue into irresponsible actions. Amen.

Think back to a time recently when you spoke rashly. If possible apologize to the person involved. Ask God's forgiveness.

■ WHEN HEARTS ARE FAINT

Psalm 142: "When my spirit grows faint within me, it is you who know my way!" (v. 3).

This prayer has been attributed to David and may have been composed while he was hiding from the wrath of King Saul in a cave. This was frightening enough, but we wonder for what David might have prayed were he facing the kind of worldwide threats that cause faint spirits today: nuclear obliteration, environmental poisoning, natural-resource depletion, population explosion. The revelation of God's redeeming love through Christ has in no way diminished such threats. The technological revolution has done far more to increase them than to control them. Jesus himself prophesied about a time when people would "faint from terror, apprehensive of what is coming on the world" (Luke 21:26). This is it, and our spirits are faint.

Whether or not our miracle-working God will deliver humanity from these potential disasters that the human family brings upon itself, we are lifted out of the murky morass of these troublesome times with the resplendent hope that our loving God knows the way. Our spirits will become faint at times in respect to "what is coming on the world." Then, "Stand firm in the faith; be men of courage; be strong" wrote Paul (1 Cor. 16:13). Our God knows the way and will bring us safely through.

 My life is short, O Lord. Strengthen my faith that I may stand firm, and may all that I do be done in love. Amen.

Memorize today's Bible verse. Repeat it when you are discouraged.

■ BACK TO MEMORIES AGAIN

Psalm 143:   "I remember the days of long ago"
(v. 5).

The psalmist did what we often do when the present is uncomfortable and the future obscure, he "remembered the days of long ago." We can never go back, but we can't help but think back—to meditate on what God has done.

The secret to making effective use of our memories is not in a redundant rehearsal of what we have done; it is in recalling and reminiscing about what God has done for us and in us. If we are candid and honest about it, we will see much that will give comfort and strength for the journey ahead. We often failed; God never failed us. We were indifferent to him, even ignored him at times; God never ceased to care for us or to be concerned about our welfare. There were times when we almost gave up on God; he has never nor will he ever give up on us.

Well then, are we less important to God now than we were in the youth and middle-age periods of our lives? If he stayed with us up to this point, do you really believe that he will abandon us now? Remember and be grateful for "the days of long ago," but let us stand tall in our faith and courageous in our commitment today, for he is truly a great God.

 I remember, Lord, and I thank you for never forgetting me. Show me the way I should go, for to you I life up my soul. Amen.

**Reminisce today about what God has done for you.
Try sharing these memories with someone near you.**

■ THE GOD WHO WALKS WITH US

Psalm 144: "Man is like a breath; his days are like a fleeting shadow" (v. 4).

We may get upset with the psalm writers when they continually remind us of our finitude. We are but a wisp of wind in the time and space of God's great universe, a smidgen of moist air or a shadow without lasting substance. How difficult it is to understand how God can regard man and woman with such high regard and show them so much concern!

Yet he who can touch the mountains, so that they smoke and send forth lightning and scatter the enemies, has reached down his hand from on high, rescued, and delivered us. He created us as the objects of his love and continues to love us, seeking to save us from destroying ourselves and the world he has placed in our hands. Even when we reject him, he reaches out to draw us back to himself. Even while he bears the painful consequences of our rebelliousness, he offers us his healing and manifests his desire to restore us to love and joy. And when we finally turn to him, there he is, ready to forgive our sins and reconcile us to his life and purposes.

This is the God who walks with us as we ease into the final years of our earthly sojourn. He is the God who will see us through that significant event that will usher us into the eternal glory and splendor of his presence. "Blessed are the people of whom this is true; blessed are the people whose God is the Lord!"

You are walking with me even as I walk with you, O Lord, and therein is the happiness that is far greater than anything this earth can offer. Amen.

Ask God to show you how you can make the most of your remaining years.

■ A MIRACLE-WORKING GOD

Psalm 147: "He heals the brokenhearted and binds up their wounds" (v. 3).

Not any of us have walked on water, and most of us have not experienced instantaneous healing as the result of prayer. And yet we believe our God is a worker of miracles. "A miracle," according to C. S. Lewis, "is emphatically not an event without cause or without results. Its cause is the activity of God; its results follow according to Natural Law." God is not a magician, but he is a miracle worker. The healing of a bloody wound, the overcoming of a vicious disease, the unfolding flower, bursting seed, bearing of fruit, conception and birth of a child, and so many other things that happen with us and about us, are miracles. Their cause is the activity of God. Because these things happen naturally, we take them for granted and neglect to regard them as miracles.

God performs the greatest miracle of all when, incarnate in Jesus Christ, "he heals the brokenhearted, and binds up their wounds." He did this for each of us; he is doing this for people around us. While not denying the incidents or divine nature of instantaneous, supernatural happenings, it is not as important to seek them as it is to claim the great miracle of our spiritual healing and to walk by faith among the uncountable, though often unrecognized, miracles that go on all the time.

 Thank you, my God, for the healing and wound-binding that you have performed in my life. I continue to abide in your blessed grace and healing power. Amen.

Think back on instances when you experienced God's healing and other "miracles." Thank God for them.

■ KEEP PRAISING HIM!

Psalm 150:   "Praise the Lord!" (v. 1).

The last five psalms in the book of Psalms all begin with the injunction to "praise the Lord." And then the psalm writer calls upon sun, moon, waters, sea creatures, fire and snow and stormy wind, mountains and hills, gardens and beasts, creeping things and flying birds, kings and peoples, men and maids and children, to offer praises unto God. He tells us how to do it: with trumpet, tambourine, and dancing, with harp and lyre, strings and flute, and loud clashing cymbals.

"Let everything that has breath praise the Lord." What a great way to wind up this little volume! This is indeed the key to happy aging—getting excited about God, loving him through loving our fellow beings, accepting this time and place as God's present vocation for us, believing in our own significance as God's sons and daughters, and spending the rest of our lives praising him in words and deeds by loving and serving others.

This will not be easy. We can do it only with divine grace, and that grace is given to every one of us. God loves us, cares about us, and entrusts to us his own Spirit, making himself dependent upon us to carry out his purposes in our world. God is with us; let us go with him.

 I praise you, Lord, for allowing me to be important to you, for putting meaning and purpose into my life, for making these final years significant and joyful despite the adversities that come with aging. Amen.

Can you think of a person with whom you could share this book?

ISN'T PERFUME wonderful, Lord? It all looks pretty much the same except for the packaging, and it's all probably made of about the same ingredients. And yet . . . one perfume can remind you of a young girl's nosegay; another scent conjures up a picture of a mysterious femme fatale; and still another makes you think of moonlight and roses.

Perfume Atomizers.

No. 8K3013

Our price.... .2€
Unreliable.

I remember when my son was about six years old and my mother often came from out of town to visit us. She always wore marvelous perfume that was expensive and extraordinary. Her clothes, her hair, even her purse had that special fragrance. Since the two of them would spend a lot of time sitting very close reading books and sharing secrets, one day I asked my son how he liked Grandma's perfume. He said, "Perfume? I just thought ALL old people smelled like that."

Like the perfume, Lord, we're all made of the same ingredients and look pretty much the same except for the packaging; and we, too, convey different images — of innocence or worldliness, romance or mystery or whatever. But wouldn't it be nice, Lord, if as we grow in age and wisdom, we could emit a happy fragrance?

Maybe it would be the fragrance of patience, the essence of experience, the aroma of time spent listening to small children and making them believe that we really care what they are saying, the scent of a life well spent.

Show us, Lord, how to live so that we will age well. Help us see each day as a potpourri of opportunities, a time to make the kind of memories that we will be able to enjoy and savor in years to come. Teach us to yearn not so much for the sweet smell of success as for the aroma of holiness.